Check and test

ICT

Anne Ramkaran

Published by BBC Educational Publishing,
BBC Worldwide, Room A3040, Woodlands, 80 Wood Lane, London W12 0TT

First published 2003   Reprinted 2005

Colour reproduction by Spectrum Colour, England

Printed and bound by Sedit, Italy

Contents

About GCSE Bitesize

GCSE Bitesize is a revision service designed to help you achieve success in your exams with books, television programmes and a website, which can be found at **www.bbc.co.uk/education/revision**. It's called Bitesize because it breaks revision into bite-sized chunks, making it easier to learn.

How to use this book

This book explains and tests the **100 essential things** you need to know to succeed in GCSE ICT. It provides:

- the key vocabulary you need in the 'Check the facts' section
- activities to test your understanding in the 'Test yourself' section.

Use this book to check your understanding of GCSE ICT. If you can prove to yourself that you're confident with these key ideas, you'll know that you're on track with your learning.

You can use this book to test yourself:

- during your GCSE course
- at the end of the course during revision.

As you revise, you can use Check and Test in several ways:

- as a summary of the essential information on each of the 100 topics to help you revise those areas
- to check your revision progress: test yourself to see how confident you are with each topic
- to keep track and plan your time:
  - you know how much time you have left in which to revise
  - you know how many topics you need to cover
  - aim to check and test a set number of topics each time you revise.

GCSE Bitesize website

The GCSE Bitesize Revision: ICT website provides even more explanation and practice to help you revise. It can be found at:
www.bbc.co.uk/education/revision

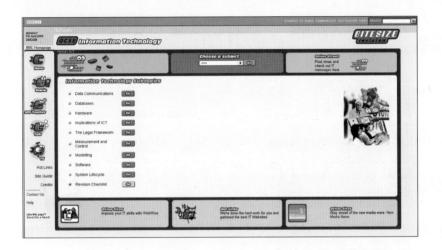

Computer systems

Check the facts

Information systems involve **input, storage, processing**
and **output. They sometimes involve feedback.**

Data moves from **input** to **processing stages**, and then to **output**. Data can
be **stored** so it can be used again.

During **input**, data is converted into an electronic form that the
computer can use.

Processing takes data and converts it into useful information ready for
output. It may involve **calculating, selecting records** and **sorting lists**.

When data is **stored**, it is written on a disk or other storage
medium. The data is still in an **electronic form**.

The **output** from an information system is the information produced for
the user. This can be a **printed report**, an **image on the screen** or
sound. Control systems output signals to actuators.

Feedback is when output affects the input data in control systems.

What happens when you type an essay?

1 Type in essay **(input)**
2 Save work on disk **(storage)**
3 Edit, centre text and embolden the title **(processing)**
4 Save your finished version **(storage)**
5 Print out a copy of your essay **(output)**

Test yourself

1 Complete the grid below to show at which stage each activity occurs.

Activity	Input	Processing	Storage	Output
Saving a spreadsheet				
Entering a customer's details				
Working out the average mark				
Producing a list of pupils on paper				

Check the facts

A **system flow chart** **is a diagram that shows the way in which** data moves through a system.

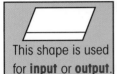

This shape is used for **input** or **output**.

This shape is used for a **process**.

This shape is used for **stored data**.

Data flows through a supermarket system when items are scanned at the checkout. **Arrows** connect the shapes and show **movement of data**.

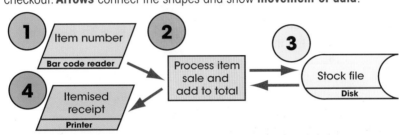

Box 1 shows that the **item code** is entered by reading the **bar code**. The **input device** is shown in the bottom section of the box.

Box 2 describes the **process** that is being carried out.

Box 3 tells us which **file** is used to find the **item data**. The item name and price are needed from the file. The arrow pointing towards the process box shows this **data transfer**. The other arrow shows that **new data** will be written to the file. The number of items in stock will be changed.

Box 4 tells us the **output** that the system will produce. The **output device** is shown in the bottom section of the box.

When you draw a system flow chart, remember:
- Input, output and storage boxes are always connected to **process boxes**, never to each other.
- Process boxes are **never connected** to other process boxes.
- Two or more processes can use the **same data store**.

Test yourself

1 What does a system flow chart show?
2 Why are two arrows needed between the process box and the storage box in the diagram above?

Computer systems

BBC GCSE Check and Test: ICT

7

Check the facts

> Data is raw facts and has no meaning on its own.
> Information always has meaning, because there is a context.
>
> **DATA + CONTEXT = INFORMATION**

An example of an item of data is **17**.

The data becomes information when put into a **context**, which makes it mean something.

The data can have a different meaning in a different context.

Data item

There are **17** pupils going on a visit to the theatre

The address is **17** Rowan Road

Context

> Computers store data. Humans understand information.

Below is part of a spreadsheet. There is data in the spreadsheet, but we don't know what it means.

	A	B	C	D
1				
2		1	8	8
3		2.73	6	16.38
4				24.38

Data items are present, but no context.

If headings are added, we provide a context and the spreadsheet now gives information.

	A	B	C	D
1	Item	Cost of item	Quantity	Value
2	Notepad	£1	8	£8
3	Calendar	£2.73	6	£16.38
4			**Total value**	£24.38

Headings and £ signs give context.

Test yourself

1 Identify three data items in the following sentence:

I bought six carrots that cost 30p.

2 Explain the difference between information and data.

Check the facts

Input devices capture data and send it into the computer system. Different input devices are used for entering different kinds of data.

- A **standard** QWERTY keyboard is used to type in text and numbers. It also has **function keys** to carry out common actions. Each key that is pressed sends a different number to the computer.

- The **application software** uses the **number** to work out the meaning of a key.

- A **concept keyboard**, or **overlay keyboard**, has keys labelled with **words** or **pictures**.

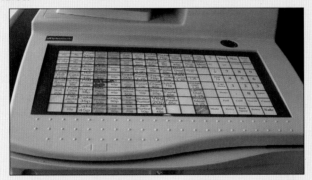

Concept, or overlay, keyboard

This photograph shows a keyboard on an **electronic till**. When a key is pressed, the software uses the number sent by the key to look up the price of the item in a file.

Overlays like this can easily be changed. The system is simple to use and faster than keying in the prices. Errors are less likely, as there is no need to remember prices. Because the keyboard is flat and waterproof, it is easy to keep clean.

Test yourself

1 Which of the following decides the meaning of a single key press?
a) The keyboard
b) The computer hardware
c) The label on the key
d) The software running on the computer

2 Give three reasons why an overlay keyboard might be used on a till.

Computer systems

BBC GCSE Check and Test: ITC

Check the facts

Computer systems use a graphical interface. The user has to be able to move a pointer around on the screen to select items, position the cursor and draw shapes.

Mouse

The mouse is the **most widely used** pointing device. Data about the amount of movement in two directions is sent to the computer.

Moving the mouse in this direction gives two sets of **directional data values**.

Up/down data

Left/right data

The data is used by the software to **position the pointer** on the screen.

The mouse on a PC has at least two buttons, while on an Apple Macintosh there is only one. Pressing a button sends a signal to the computer. The software works out what the signal means. Pressing the left button usually selects an object or starts an action.

Trackerball

A trackerball is another pointing device. It is a ball mounted over a pair of rollers. The user moves the ball and, as the rollers turn, **directional data** is sent to the computer. The trackerball uses **less space than a mouse** and is sometimes built into notebook computers.

Touchpad

A touchpad allows the user to move the screen pointer by **moving a finger over the pad**. There are two buttons, corresponding to the mouse buttons. Touchpads are also used on notebook computers.

Test yourself

1 Explain why holding down the left mouse button while moving the mouse selects text in a word-processing package, but the same action draws a shape in a graphics package.

2 Why is a touchpad more suitable than a mouse on a notebook computer?

Computer systems

Check the facts

> **Input devices need to suit the location and the type of data to be input.**

Touch screens

A touch screen is both an **input** and an **output** device. Choices are displayed on the screen and selected by touching the screen with a finger. The point of contact is detected and **coordinate data** is transmitted to the computer. The data is used to work out what action to take.

Touch screens are often used in **fast food restaurants**. The layout is simple to change and the screen is easy to use and keep clean. Space is saved, because only one device is needed for both input and output.

Light pens

A light pen is placed against an ordinary screen and its position is detected. The pen could be used to select a choice from a menu or to draw a line.

Digitisers

Digitisers are used to **input drawings**. The picture is 'drawn' on its flat surface. The digitiser transmits **position data** to the computer, and the data is used to construct the drawing on screen.

Test yourself

1 Choose the best input device for each application:

   a) drawing a map by hand

   b) entering meals chosen in a fast food restaurant.

Check the facts

Scanners **and** digital cameras **are used to capture image data.**

Scanners

Scanners detect the **colour of light** reflected from a picture. They transmit this data to the computer.

The colour of lots of **separate dots** is detected as the scanner works across the picture.

Scanner resolution = number of dots per inch

Scanner **software** lets the user choose the resolution and the type of scan. Scans can be colour or black and white.

The scanned image can be saved in a graphics file for use with other computer software.

Digital cameras

Digital cameras store a **digital image** when a picture is taken. The resolution is given in **megapixels**.

Megapixels = number of dots in the image

Pictures can be viewed straight away and stored. The image data can be transferred to a computer using a **cable** or **docking station**. Some cameras can save images on a floppy disk or mini-CD.

Test yourself

1 What device would you use to input a copy of a picture to a computer?

2 Pictures showing pupil activities are needed for a school magazine. Give two advantages and two disadvantages of using a digital camera rather than an ordinary camera to take these pictures.

Computer systems

Check the facts

> Microphones **and electronic keyboards are used to input sound.** Speakers **are used to output sound.**

Any kind of sound can be captured using a **microphone**. Data is collected about the **amplitude** (loudness) and **frequency** (pitch) of the sound.

Sound data can be used in many ways. For example, it can be used with **speech recognition software** to produce text in a word-processed document. It can also be saved and used to provide sounds for **presentations** or **web pages**.

Sounds are **sampled** many times a second to produce enough digital data to rebuild the sound accurately when the data is sent to the speaker.

Computer systems often have **built-in speakers**. However, you can output a better-quality sound by using better-quality speakers.

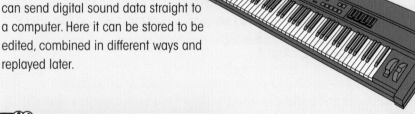

Electronic **musical keyboards** can send digital sound data straight to a computer. Here it can be stored to be edited, combined in different ways and replayed later.

Computer systems

Test yourself

1 Name two devices that can be used to input sound data into a computer system.

2 What device would you use to capture the sound of a choir singing?

3 Give two different ways in which spoken sound data can be used.

Check the facts

> Screens are used to display information. Most computer systems have some kind of screen display.

Screens must be suitable for the situation in which they are to be used.

Screen displays can be **colour** or **monochrome**. Desktop computers and notebook computers have colour displays. Displays on other computer systems are often monochrome and can be quite small.

Screens are measured **diagonally**, from top left to bottom right. On a **Cathode Ray Tube (CRT) screen**, the visible area is smaller than the actual area of the screen.

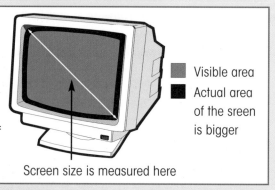

■ Visible area
■ Actual area of the sreen is bigger

Screen size is measured here

CRT screens work the same way as TV screens. They are heavy and take up a lot of space.

Liquid Crystal Display (LCD) screens are light and take up little space. They can be used with a desktop computer. Notebook computers also use this kind of screen.

Display screens used for certain applications need to be protected. Cash-point machines and displays at railway stations need to be resistant to damage.

Test yourself

1 Match the three screen types to the situations:

   a) Monochrome 9" CRT

   b) Colour 14" LCD

   c) Colour 19" CRT

   i) Display for a shop till

   ii) Display for a desktop computer

   iii) Display for a notebook computer.

2 George buys a CRT screen. The viewable size is 15", but the box is labelled 17". Explain why both measurements are correct.

Computer systems

www.bbc.co.uk/revision

Check the facts

> Printers produce output on paper. There are several different types of printers.

Dot-matrix printers are **impact** printers. They produce output when an ink-coated ribbon is pressed hard against the paper. These printers are used to produce identical copies of data on **multi-part documents**. Invoices and delivery notes are produced in this way.

Ink-jet and **laser printers** are **non-impact** printers. Ink-jet printers spray **liquid ink** onto the paper. Laser printers use **toner powder**, which is heated to bind it onto the paper.

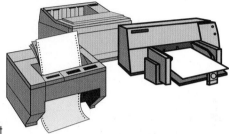

Printers differ in cost and in cost per printed page. The quality of output and speed also varies.

Printer type	Method of printing	Cost of printer	Cost per page	Colour	Speed	Quality of output
Colour ink-jet	Liquid ink (black and three colours)	Low	High	Yes	Slow	Medium
Mono ink-jet	Liquid ink	Very low	Medium	No	Quite slow	Medium
Dot matrix	Inked ribbon	Low	Low	Not usually	Slow	Low
Mono laser	Toner	Medium	Medium	No	Fast	High
Colour laser	Toner (black and three colours)	High	High	Yes	Fast	High

When choosing a printer for an application, **speed**, **cost** and **quality** are important considerations.

Test yourself

1 State, with reasons, the type of printer that you would choose for each of the following tasks:

a) producing six hundred copies of a black-and-white newsletter

b) producing invoices and delivery notes

c) producing five copies of a colour poster to advertise a school team trial.

Computer systems

Check the facts

> The same units are used for computer memory and all types of storage media.

The smallest storage unit is the **bit**. This holds a **single binary digit**, 0 or 1.

> **A byte contains eight bits.**

Unit	Description	Number of bytes
Byte	Eight bits, a byte holds one character	1
Kilobyte	2^{10} bytes, approximately a thousand bytes	1024
Megabyte	2^{10} kilobytes, approximately one million bytes	1048576
Gigabyte	2^{10} megabytes, approximately a thousand million bytes	1073741824

Memory is the **Immediate Access Store** inside the computer. There are two types of memory:

1) **RAM** is **Random Access Memory**. The contents of RAM can be changed by the user, but are lost when the computer is switched off because **RAM is volatile**.

RAM is used to hold **user programs** and **data**.
If you use a **spreadsheet**, the program instructions are placed in RAM. The data you type in is also kept in RAM.

2) **ROM** is **Read Only Memory**. Its contents can't be changed by the user. It is **non-volatile** and does not lose its contents when the computer is switched off.

ROM is used to hold the **instructions** needed to start up the computer system and load the operating system.

Test yourself

1 Give two differences between ROM and RAM.

2 Why does a computer system need to have ROM?

3 Give two uses of RAM.

Check the facts

Magnetic disks **are the most widely used media for storing data. Data is stored by** magnetising tiny spots on the surface. **Floppy disks and hard disks are both magnetic.**

Floppy disks	Hard disks
Made of **plastic**.	Made of **metal**.
Can hold **1.44 megabytes** of data.	Can hold much more data than a floppy disk. Capacity is measured in gigabytes (e.g. 40 **gigabytes**).
Have to be put into a **floppy-disk drive**.	
Disks are **exchangeable** and can be moved from one computer to another.	Are built into the **hard-disk drive** of the computer.
	Disks are **not exchangeable**.
Reading and writing of data is **slow**.	Reading and writing of data is **fast**.

Floppy disks are mostly used to **hold files** being moved from one system to another.

Hard disks are used to hold all the **operating system programs** and **application programs** required on a computer. They also hold **data files** produced by the user.

Data is arranged in the same way on all magnetic disks. The data is written along **circular tracks**. The tracks are divided into sectors by inter-sector gaps that do not contain data.

Test yourself

1 How is data arranged on a hard disk?

2 Draw a chart like the one below and give three differences between a hard disk and a floppy disk:

Hard	Floppy

Computer systems

Check the facts

There are two types of magnetic tape:
1) tape on a large spool
2) tape on a cassette.

Tape is a **serial storage medium**. Data must be read from the start to the end of the tape. To read the last record in a file requires all the other records to be read first.

Spools of tape are still used to store data for some batch-processing applications on large computer systems. Tape has a **high capacity** and both reading and writing are fast. **Payroll** is an example of an application that may use magnetic tape.

Tapes on cassette are used in special tape drives to make **backup copies** of all the data on a hard disk. These tapes have a very high capacity. Reading and writing data is fast, so it doesn't take too long to back up several gigabytes of data. More importantly, the tapes can be **removed and stored in a safe place**.

Tape is not a suitable storage medium for data files where direct access to records in different parts of the file is required.

Test yourself

1 Give three reasons why magnetic tape is used to back up the hard disk.

2 Magnetic tape is a serial storage medium. What does this mean?

Check the facts

> **CD-ROM, CD-R, CD-RW, DVD-RAM and DVD-ROM are all optical disks. Data is stored by altering the reflective properties of the disk surface.**

CD-ROM and DVD are both used by software houses to supply applications software.

CDs

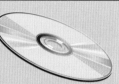

CD-ROM is a **read-only** medium. The data is put on the CD-ROM when it is made. No changes can be made.

CD-R is a medium that can have **user data written onto it**. The process of writing is called **burning**. Once data has been written to the disk, the data can't be changed, but more data can be added if there is space. CD-R can be used to hold archive and backup copies of files. A CD-writer drive is needed to write data. The disk can be read in any CD drive.

CD-RW is a **rewritable disk**. This means that user data can be written onto the CD and then changed, deleted or overwritten as often as necessary. It is an **exchangeable medium** and can be used in the same way as a floppy disk. A **CD-writer drive** is needed to write the data, but the disk can be read in any CD or DVD drive.

DVDs

DVD-ROM is a **read-only medium**. DVD-ROM can hold much more data than CD-ROM.

DVD-RAM is a DVD that can be **rewritten** many times.

Test yourself

1 Which optical disk has the highest capacity?

2 Give one use for CD-ROM.

3 Explain the difference between CD-R and CD-RW.

Computer systems

BBC GCSE Check and Test: ICT

Check the facts

> The operating system provides a link between the application software and the hardware of the computer system.

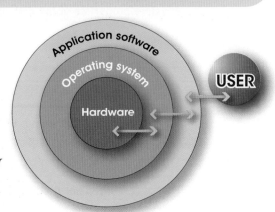

This diagram shows how the operating system forms a layer between the application software and the hardware. The user interacts mainly with the application software.

The operating system manages **system resources**. It allocates **memory** for application programs and data. It also allocates **processor time** to different tasks.

System security and **data transfers** are both managed by the operating system.

Data transfers

The operating system has to **allocate disk space** and **update the directory information** when files are saved. It has to **allocate space in memory** when blocks of data are read from the disk.

When an application sends a job to the printer, the operating system has to **transfer the data**. Printers are slower than computers, so the operating system has to check the printer is ready before sending each batch of data.

The operating system receives **input data from the keyboard** and **mouse** and passes it on to the application software.

Test yourself

1 What is linked by the operating system?

2 List four tasks that are carried out by the operating system.

3 Why is the user not aware of what the operating system is doing?

Check the facts

> **A multi-tasking system is one that appears to run more than one application program at a time.**

The multi-tasking system has different programs running in different areas of memory. Each program is given a **priority**.

A system could have a word-processing program running as the **highest priority**. A label-printing program could be running with a **lower priority**.

There's not much I can't do!

The word-processing program will mostly be waiting for the user to press the next key. During such times, the label-printing program can send data to the printer. As soon as the word-processing program needs processor time, the label-printing program stops and waits.

Multi-tasking gets both jobs done, apparently at the same time.

Multi-tasking works because the central processing unit of a computer can carry out **millions of instructions every second**. Peripherals, such as printers, are slower, and humans are extremely slow by comparison.

A multi-tasking operating system must be able to set up **partitions in memory** for the different tasks. It must also be able to keep the data for the different tasks separate.

The operating system must be able to **handle the priorities** given to the different tasks.

Test yourself

1 What is a multi-tasking system?

2 State three actions that a multi-tasking operating system must be able to do.

Computer systems

BBC GCSE Check and Test: ICT

Check the facts

A **multi-user system** allows many different users to run their chosen applications apparently at the same time. Each user will appear to be the only person using the system.

The operating system allocates a **very small slice of processor time** to each user in turn. Switching between users is so fast that most do not notice a delay.

start

Starting with 1, each user gets a segment of processor time in turn.

The operating system must be able to switch **user programs** and **data** in and out of memory quickly.

The system must be able to **keep track of which programs and data belong to each user**.

This type of system can make **processing power available to many users**. The computer is usually very large.

Test yourself

1 What is a multi-user system?

2 What must a multi-user operating system be able to do?

Computer systems

Check the facts

The **format** of a file is the way in which it is structured. Files of a particular format are given the **same** file name extension.

Graphics files

If a file is called **mypicture.jpg**, the file is a graphics file in **.jpg** format. The file has to be saved in the correct format; simply changing the name does not change the format.

Other standard graphics formats include **.bmp**, **.tif** and **.gif**.

A file with an **.ico** extension is an **icon graphic file**.

Files in **.bmp**, **.tif**, **.gif** or **.ico** formats can be handled by almost all application packages capable of handling graphics.

Text files

Text files can be transferred in the same way. The document must be saved as **text only** and will have a **.txt** extension.

Sound files

A standard format for sound files is **.wav**.

Data files

Data files for use in **spreadsheets** and **databases** can be transferred in a standard format. The data must be saved as a **.csv** file. The **.csv** file contains the data with commas between the values. This type of file can be imported into a spreadsheet or database.

Test yourself

1 Give two standard formats that can be used for graphics files.

2 How can data in a spreadsheet package be transferred to a database package?

3 Why isn't it a good idea to use a **.wav** extension when saving a text file?

BBC GCSE Check and Test: ICT

Computer systems

Check the facts

> The **user interface** is the way in which the user interacts with the computer. The **screen display** is a very important part of the interface.

A **command-driven interface** is shown below.

```
C: \WINDOWS > cd C: \

C: \ >md pictures

C: \ >_
```

Command to change the current directory

Command to make a new directory called 'Pictures'

Command prompt: the system is waiting for another command

Notice the **command prompt** in this interface. The user has to type in a **valid command**.

The interface is difficult to use because the commands have to be remembered.

Command interfaces are **fast**, because the computer does not have to manage a complicated graphics display.

Command interfaces make little demand on **memory** and **disk space**. The system software needed to handle the interface does not take up much space.

Test yourself

1 What are the main features of a command-driven interface?

2 Give two advantages and one disadvantage of using a command-driven interface for a database application.

Check the facts

A **menu-driven interface** gives the user a series of choices. It is usually a **text-only** interface.

There can be **several menus** within an application.

Library Management System
Select the section you want to use

→ Heading and instructions

1. Loans
2. Returns
3. Catalogue update
4. Catalogue search
5. Member update
6. Exit

→ Menu choices

The user decides on the choice and types in the number. The package then moves to the correct section. There can be several menus within an application.

Advantages

1 A well-constructed menu-driven interface is **easy to use**. The number of choices that can be made is limited.

2 **No mouse is required**, so the interface can be used in applications such as cash machines, where a keypad is the usual input device.

3 The interface **makes little demand on system resources**, as it does not use a complex graphics display.

Disadvantages

1 Multiple menus can be **slow** for the user to navigate, especially if frequently performed tasks are in different branches of the menu system.

2 The user has to **remember where to find tasks** within the menu system.

Test yourself

1 Describe the main features of a menu-driven interface.

2 Give an example of an application where a menu-driven interface would be appropriate.

Check the facts

> A graphical user interface (GUI) uses windows, icons, menus and a pointing device. The user can see all the available options immediately.

Computer systems

Icons

Menu items

Window

Pointer

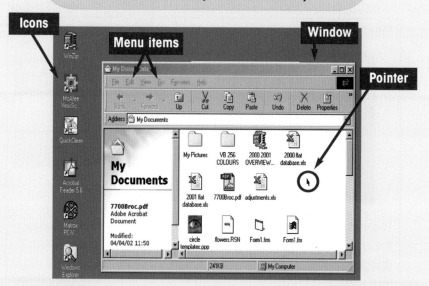

Navigation

The interface is easy to use because navigation is done by pointing and clicking a mouse. The user doesn't need to remember commands. Help is usually available.

> Navigation of most applications works in the same way, so learning a new package is fairly easy:
> • The **pull-down menus** follow a similar pattern in all packages.
> • The **mouse** selects and starts all applications in the same way.

Graphical interfaces make heavy demands on system resources. The operating system needs a lot of **disk space** and **memory**. A great deal of processor time is spent on maintaining the complex screen display.

Test yourself

1 List the main components of a graphical user interface.

2 Give two reasons why an inexperienced user may find a graphical interface easy to use.

3 Give two possible disadvantages of a graphical user interface.

Check the facts

> When designing a user interface, it is important to consider the purpose **for which it will be used** and the **level of user skill**.

There are some basic principles to follow:

The interface must be **consistent**. It must look the same and work the same throughout the application.

Important items, such as messages to the user, should appear in the **middle of the screen**, because they will be easy to see.

There should be a good **contrast** between **text** and **background colours**, so text is easy to read.

The **colour scheme** must be appropriate for the application. Pale, restful colours work best if the interface is to be used for long periods.

Consider the needs of users who experience **epilepsy** or **colour blindness**. Do not use flashing objects and avoid red/green and blue/yellow combinations.

Sound can be useful to alert users to errors, but too much sound can be distracting.

Help should be easily available, and the **help topics** should be explained in language that the user will understand.

Test yourself

1 Interface design is influenced by purpose and level of user skill.
   a) Explain how purpose might influence the choice of colour scheme.
   b) Explain how the level of user skill will influence the construction of help files.

2 Where should error messages be positioned? Why?

3 What health problems must be considered when designing an interface?

The system life cycle

Check the facts

> Every information system goes through a series of stages during its existence. These stages make up the **system life cycle**.

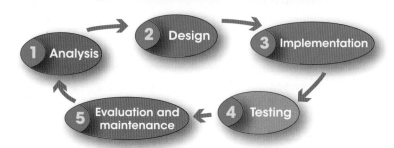

1. Analysis
2. Design
3. Implementation
4. Testing
5. Evaluation and maintenance

1 The life cycle of a new system starts with **analysis**. In this stage, the requirements are worked out.

2 Next is the **design stage**, when plans are made for the new system.

3 **Implementation** is when the system is built.

4 When the system is complete, it has to be **tested** before it can be used.

5 The **evaluation stage** is checking how well the system works. There may be small problems that can be fixed. This is **maintenance**.

Eventually, a point is reached where fixing problems isn't practical and a **new system** is needed, so the life cycle starts again.

Test yourself

1 List the stages of the system life cycle in the correct order.

2 Why does the system life cycle start again?

Check the facts

Systems analysis is the process of finding out how an existing system works and what is required of a new system if it is to solve all the end-user's problems.

There are three main ways of finding out about the present system:

1 Observe the way in which the system works.
- Find out how data moves through the system.
- Look at the documents used in the system.
- Identify any problems in the way in which the system works.

This lets you see what really happens and what data is used.
It takes a long time.

2 Interview the people who work with the system.
- Ask questions about problems with the existing system and what is expected of the new system.

This lets you explore areas of the system in detail. It also takes a long time.

3 Use **questionnaires** to collect the views of users.
- Work out all the questions and hand out forms.

This method is fast for collecting lots of ideas, although not all forms will be returned.

When the investigation is complete, list the requirements for the new system to be a success. This is called a **requirements specification** or **set of performance criteria**.

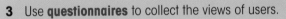

Test yourself

1 Describe the methods used in systems analysis, their advantages and disadvantages.

2 What should be produced at the end of analysis?

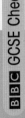

System life cycle

BBC GCSE Check and Test: ICT

Check the facts

System life cycle

> The design for a system provides all the detail necessary for the system to be **implemented** and tested.

A design should include:

1 Designs for **all the outputs** from the system. These will include screen layouts and designs for everything that will be printed. The designs need a lot of detail. Information about colour, font type and font size should be included, as well as sketches of what the outputs will look like.

2 Designs for **record structures** for databases. These will include files, fields, field types, lengths and validation methods. Primary key fields will be identified.

3 Designs for any **input forms** or **data capture forms**.

4 Designs for the **processing** that will take place, including designs for database queries and spreadsheet formulae.

Testing plans, using test data, should be made during the design stage. If designed at this stage, the tests will **check that the whole system works**. Anything left out will result in a test being failed.

Test yourself

1 Which of the following happen during the design stage:

  a) entering data into a database

  b) working out a record structure

  c) interviewing users

  d) checking how well the system works

  e) planning the layout of a poster?

2 Why should tests be planned at the design stage?

Check the facts

> **Implementation is the process of producing the required system.**

Implementation includes activities such as making **template pages** for a magazine. The template contains fixed information to appear in every issue, while stories and pictures for an individual edition will go in later, when the system is used.

Any **database record structures** are defined in the database management package.

Input forms for entering data are made and the **queries** needed to find the required records are set up.

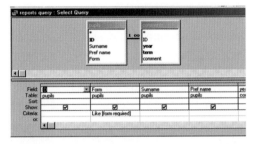

Setting up a database query during implementation

Any printed reports from a database system are produced in the database package or as **mail-merged documents** in a word-processing package.

If the system includes **spreadsheets**, these must be set up with all the headings and formulae in place, and with spaces for the user to enter his or her data.

Test yourself

1 What is implementation?

2 Describe four different tasks that might be carried out during implementation of a system for managing a video library.

Check the facts

System life cycle

In the testing stage, the testing plan is followed carefully so that the whole system is tested to make sure the requirements specification has been met.

The **test data** is put into the system and all the **outputs** are checked to make sure they are as expected.

Testing with **typical** data makes sure the system works with data that it should handle.

Testing with **extreme** data makes sure that limits are set correctly.

Testing with **erroneous** (incorrect) data checks that the system does not use the data and rejects it in a sensible way.

The table below shows the data we could use to test a **range check** (see page 42) designed to accept values between 0 and 75.

Data	What it tests	What should happen
52	To find out if typical data will be accepted	accepted
0	To find out if the lowest possible mark is accepted	accepted
75	To find out if the highest possible mark is accepted	accepted
−1	To find out if a mark below the allowed range is rejected	rejected
76	To find out if a mark above the allowed range is rejected	rejected
A	To find out if letters are rejected	rejected

Test yourself

1 Name the three types of testing that should be carried out.

2 Give a set of test data that you would use to test the input of answers in the range A to E. Explain why each data item is needed.

Check the facts

Evaluation is examining how well a system meets the requirements of the user. New systems are evaluated to find out how successful they are. Older systems are evaluated to find out if they still meet user requirements.

Evaluation criteria

Evaluation should be carried out by working through a list of **evaluation criteria**.

The criteria are based on the **performance criteria** from the analysis stage. They must cover desirable features, such as ease of use, as well as making sure the system does everything it should.

Evaluation should produce more than just **yes/no answers**. It should be a judgement of how well the system performs each task.

End users should be involved in the evaluation process. Their view of the system is very important, because they will be the people who work with the system. If they don't like it, the system will fail.

Evaluation is not limited to systems that have just been developed. It can be used when **deciding which package to buy**. Evaluation criteria can be written and the available packages can be judged against the criteria.

Test yourself

1 What is evaluation?

2 Why is evaluation carried out?

3 Why should end users be involved in the evaluation process?

Check the facts

System life cycle

All software needs to undergo maintenance during its life, so it can meet user requirements. Software undergoes three kinds of maintenance: corrective, perfective and adaptive.

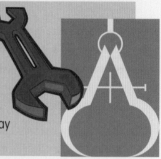

Corrective maintenance is carried out to correct problems and faults that stop the software working properly. Most problems are found and fixed during testing. However, modern packages are complex and some faults don't show up until later. There are faults that only appear when the package is used in a certain way or with certain other software.

Perfective maintenance is carried out to make the system work more efficiently. This can include making it carry out tasks faster than before.

Adaptive maintenance is carried out to make the system do extra things that it was not designed to do. This kind of maintenance is needed if user requirements change. Adaptive maintenance was carried out to allow some application software to handle the euro.

Test yourself

1 Why is maintenance of software carried out?

2 What are the three types of maintenance?

3 A software package has just been installed in an office. The staff notice that the package stops working whenever they open another package at the same time. What type of maintenance is needed?

4 Which type of maintenance can make a package carry out tasks that it was not designed to do?

Check the facts

The documentation needed with an information system is divided into two types. Technical documentation explains how the system works. User documentation provides instructions for the person using the system.

Technical documentation

The technical documentation is written for the people who will maintain the system.

It should include:

- details of the structure of every file used
- details of all the processing that can be done – database query designs and spreadsheet formulae must be included here
- samples of outputs that can be produced
- the testing plan, test data and expected results, so tests can be repeated if changes are made
- installation instructions, so the software can be installed correctly on the computers.

User documentation

User documentation provides **instructions** for the user, so it needs to be written in language that the user can understand.

It should contain:

- start-up instructions
- instructions for normal use of the system, divided into sensible sections and illustrated with screen pictures
- backup and recovery instructions
- possible problems, and what to do about them.

Test yourself

1 What is the purpose of technical documentation? List three items that should be included.

2 What three topics should be included in a user guide?

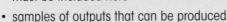

System life cycle

BBC GCSE Check and Test: ICT

Data entry

Check the facts

> A data capture form **is used to** collect data **ready for** manual input **into a computer system.**

- Data capture forms must be **organised** in the order in which data will be entered.

- The form must be **easy to fill in**. Instructions must be clear.

- There must be **enough space** for the longest possible data item at each point on the form.

- If a specific format is required (e.g. for a date), **it must be clear**.

People filling in the form will need guidance about the number of characters that can be used for each response. Using boxes for each possible character helps prevent inappropriate answers to questions.

Fill in this form in BLOCK CAPITALS. ◄── Instructions are clear

Surname ☐☐☐☐☐☐☐☐☐☐☐☐☐☐

Prompt, to ask for data

Boxes limit what can be written

- The form must **indicate any boxes that should not be filled in**.

- If the data being collected is **personal**, the uses to which it will be put should be stated.

Test yourself

1 Design a form to collect the following data: title, surname, date of birth, telephone number and address, including town and postcode. This data is needed by a book club to send news and offers to members.

2 Why is it better to use boxes (to be filled in with letters or numbers) than to draw a line on which people write?

Check the facts

> Data is captured as black marks made in specific places on pre-printed forms.

 Optical Mark Recognition (OMR) forms are **easy to fill in**. A **black mark** is made in the required place.

 All the printing on the form is in **ink that will not be detected** by the reading machine.

 The reading process is **fast** and **accurate**.

 The machine **detects marks** and then **transmits data** about their location. This data is then used by the application software.

 Forms can be collected and **processed as a batch** or they can be **processed one at a time**.

Applications

Applications for OMR include:

- recording, inputting and marking answers to multiple-choice examination papers

  (data entry is fast and accurate and the computer adds up the marks)

- recording and entering National Lottery selections

  (the form is easy to fill in, data entry is very fast and a receipt can be produced straight away).

Sometimes forms can't be read or extra marks have been made. These forms are rejected and the data must be put onto a new form or entered manually.

Test yourself

1 What is OMR and how does it work?

2 Why is OMR used to input and mark multiple-choice papers?

Data entry

Data entry

Check the facts

> An **Optical Character Reader (OCR)** detects the pattern of light and dark areas on a scanned document and converts these patterns to **character codes**.

The OCR software matches the patterns detected by the reader against stored character patterns. The character codes are built up into text in the computer memory.

Uses

• OCR is used to read **postcodes** on envelopes. The postcode is then converted to a magnetic strip.

• Data from **turn-around documents**, such as **electricity bills**, is read using OCR.

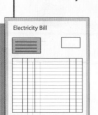

The account number is read when the bill is paid. This avoids transposition errors that can occur when long numbers are entered manually. It is also faster than typing in the number.

• OCR can also be used to input any **printed text**. Most scanners come with OCR software.

The software converts the scanned image of a page of text into a text file.

OCR systems can recognise a wide range of **standard fonts**, but most find it difficult to recognise handwriting, because it varies too much.

Test yourself

1 What is OCR and how does it work?

2 Give two reasons why OCR is used to input account numbers from electricity bills rather than using a manual method.

3 Why does handwriting present a problem to OCR systems?

Check the facts

> **Magnetic Ink Character Recognition (MICR) is used in bank cheque processing because it provides a high level of security.**

For 24 hour Telephone Ba

Magnetic ink is used to print account numbers and sort code numbers along the bottom of the cheque before it is issued to the customer.

size Bank, Hillside, Little Widton

Account Payee

The **character set** is specially designed for the purpose and contains only digits and a few separating characters.

/02
heque Number   Sort Code   Account Number

⑆003800⑆ 09⑈0800⑉ 1845 4

Data entry

- When the cheque is paid into a bank, the amount is added using a special **magnetic ink printer**.
- Cheques are all sent to **one centre** for processing.
- When the data is read, the ink is **magnetised** and the magnetic pattern is detected.
- Characters are identified by **matching the pattern** of magnetisation with stored patterns.
- The method is **secure**, because any attempt to change account details in ordinary ink is just ignored.
- The reading process is **very fast**, much faster than OCR, because of the small number of patterns to be compared.

Test yourself

1 What is MICR?

2 Why is MICR used rather than OCR for processing cheques?

BBC GCSE Check and Test: ICT

Check the facts

> Bar codes are read by a **bar code scanner**. The amount of light reflected by the dark and light bands is detected. A bar code holds a **single piece of data**, **usually a number**.

- Different widths of **dark and light bands** represent different characters. The bar code can be read from either end.

- Bar codes provide a **fast, accurate method** of entering a small amount of data. They are used to input item numbers in **supermarket point-of-sale systems**. The item number is then used to find the item record in a file. The price and description are retrieved and printed on the itemised receipt.

- Bar codes are also used in **libraries** to input book numbers and borrower numbers for loan systems.

- Bar codes are easy to print and bar-coded labels are used to **track parcels** in the postal system.

Errors

Errors do occur when reading bar codes. The printed bar code may be smudged or dirty. If the code can't be read, the number, which is printed with the code, is input manually.

Test yourself

1 A supermarket uses bar codes to input item data at the checkout.

a) What data is input about each item?

b) Explain how this data allows an itemised receipt to be produced.

c) Sometimes a bar code cannot be read. How does the till operator deal with this problem?

Check the facts

> A **magnetic strip** is used to hold a very small amount of data on a plastic card. **Smart cards** look the same as magnetic strip cards, but they have **memory** built into the card. This allows data to be **written** as well as **read**.

Magnetic strip cards

- The magnetic strip is put on the card when it is made. The data is written onto the card by putting a **magnetic code** onto the strip.

- The card reader detects the magnetic pattern and **converts this to a number**.

- Magnetic strip cards are widely used. Applications include **bank cards**, **library cards** and **swipe cards** to open door locks in hotels or other buildings.

- The magnetised strip can be damaged by heat or bending the card. Exposing the card to a magnetic field will change the magnetic pattern of the data, making the card unreadable.

Smart cards

Smart cards are replacing magnetic strip cards. Because they can have new data written to them, they are used for **loyalty point schemes**. The card can hold much more data than a simple magnetic strip card.

Test yourself

1 How is data stored on a magnetic strip card?

2 Give two differences between a magnetic strip card and a smart card.

3 How can data on a magnetic strip card be lost?

Data entry

BBC GCSE Check and Test: ICT

Data entry

Check the facts

> Data validation **is making sure that data entered into the computer is** sensible **and** reasonable.

Data validation is carried out by the **computer**, not the user. It ensures that:

- data can be used by the application software
- the data is sensible.

1 Range check

Validation cannot make sure data is correct. For example, if an exam mark is validated to make sure it is in the range of 0 to 100 and the user types in 36 instead of 63, the mark will be valid, even though it is wrong.

This kind of validation, used to make sure that data is inside a fixed set of values, is called a **range check**.

A range check can be carried out on letters as well as numbers. For example, it could make sure that a letter entered is in the range of A to E. So, if the user typed in F, it would be rejected.

2 Presence check

A presence check makes sure **data has been entered**. If the space for entering data in a required field has been left empty, the check will not accept the record.

3 Data-type check

This makes sure that **data entered matches the type of data required**. It will find errors, such as putting text into a number field.

Test yourself

1 What is data validation?

2 Why is valid data not always correct data?

3 Explain how a range check works.

Check the facts

> Check digits are used to validate numeric data, such as account numbers and numbers read from bar codes and magnetic strips.

The check digit is a **single digit** calculated from the rest of the digits in the data. It is attached to the end of the data when it is stored. The check digit will therefore be at the **end of the bar code**.

When a bar code is read, the check digit is recalculated and compared with the **check digit in the bar code**. If they match, the data is valid. If they don't match, the bar code has not been scanned correctly and the error must be corrected.

The calculation used for producing the check digit can vary, but the same method must be used when the check digit is first calculated and when it is recalculated.

Check digits can find **transposition errors** in account numbers, because changing the position of digits gives a different answer.

Data entry

The method used for calculating a check digit is shown below:

1	8	4	0	2	8	1	1	0	3

The calculation is done by multiplying each digit, except the check digit, by the amount shown.

This is the check digit ↑

1	8	4	0	2	8	1	1	0	3
x1	x2	x3	x4	x5	x6	x7	x8	x9	
=1	=16	=12	=0	=10	=48	=7	=8	=0	

Now add up the answers.   Total=102

Divide the total by 11 and the remainder is the check digit.

| 102 divided by 11 = 9 with a remainder of 3 | The check digit is 3. |

Test yourself

1 What is a check digit and how is it used to validate a bar code number?

2 Why does changing the position of digits in a number change the check digit calculated?

Check the facts

> **A verification check is designed to make sure that** data has been transferred correctly from one medium to another. Data is often verified **when it is entered.**

Verification can be done by **typing in data twice** and comparing the two versions. If they are not the same, the user has to correct the error by referring to the original source document.

Very simple verification happens when the user is asked by the computer to **confirm an action**.

The window below shows how the system checks that the user really intends to close a document without saving it first.

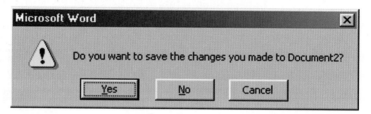

Batch totals

Another verification check is the use of **batch totals**. If you count up the number of records that have to be entered and check this against the number of records actually entered, mistakes will be found, such as **missing out a record** or **entering an extra record**.

Test yourself

1 What is the purpose of a verification check?

2 Give two examples of verification checks and describe the type of mistake that each will find.

Data entry

Check the facts

> Parity checking **makes sure that** data has been transferred correctly from one medium to another. **It is mainly used to check data as it is transferred over communication lines. It can also be used to check data transferred from backing store to memory.**

Parity checking detects corruption of data by **checking that the binary digits have not been changed** during the transfer of each byte.

Each character code is transferred together with a **parity bit**. This can be done because a **byte** has **eight bits**, but the code for the standard character set uses just **seven bits**.

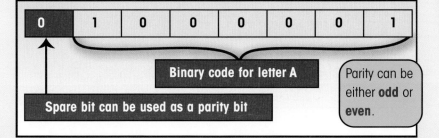

| 0 | 1 | 0 | 0 | 0 | 0 | 0 | 1 |

Binary code for letter A

Parity can be either **odd** or **even**.

Spare bit can be used as a parity bit

If parity is **odd**, the parity bit is set so that the **total number of 1s** in the byte is an **odd number**.

If parity is **even**, the parity bit is set so that the **total number of 1s** in the byte is an **even number**.

Any change in a single bit in the byte will be detected, because the parity bit setting will not be correct.

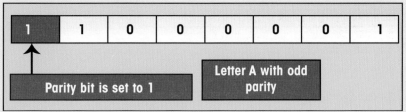

| 1 | 1 | 0 | 0 | 0 | 0 | 0 | 1 |

Parity bit is set to 1

Letter A with odd parity

Test yourself

1 When is parity checking used?

2 What kind of error does a parity check find?

Data entry

Check the facts

Data logging is collecting data from sensors and storing it for processing.

Sensors detect **environmental conditions**, such as heat, pressure and light. The sensor will transmit an **analogue signal** to an analogue-to-digital converter. This sends a digital value to the computer. The computer cannot handle analogue data.

Signals from the sensor must be **calibrated** to a known scale before the sensor is used, otherwise the results will not make sense.

For example:

To calibrate a temperature sensor, we could place it in ice at 0 °C and read the sensor value. We now know that this sensor reading is equivalent to 0 °C. We repeat this process using boiling water at 100 °C, and the computer uses the two readings to work out the temperature that corresponds to each heat sensor reading.

Sensors work within a **certain value range** and to **different levels of accuracy**. Different heat sensors are needed to measure change in body temperature to those used to monitor the temperature in a furnace.

Test yourself

1 Give three different environmental conditions that can be measured by sensors.

2 Why is the analogue sensor signal converted to a digital value?

3 What is calibration?

4 Why is calibration necessary?

5 How would a temperature sensor be calibrated?

Check the facts

> Data is collected from sensors at **regular intervals**.
> The data can be collected for varying lengths of time.

Logging interval

> **Logging interval** = the time between readings

The time between readings depends on the **rate at which changes occur**.

Logging temperature data during a chemical reaction needs a short logging interval (e.g. 0.01 seconds), because change takes place rapidly. Weather data can be collected with a much longer logging interval, because change is less rapid.

Logging period

> **Logging period** = the time over which data is collected

Measurements can be made for long periods to record long-term changes, such as climate. Other changes are completed quickly, and data does not have to be collected for as long.

Sensors

Sensors can be **connected directly to the computer**, where the data is to be stored and processed, but this is not always possible. Remote data-logging equipment can collect the data and then transmit the readings using **communication links**.

Weather data is often transmitted in this way.

Weather station with sensors

Computer will process logged data

Data entry

BBC GCSE Check and Test: ICT

Test yourself

1 Explain what is meant by **(a)** logging interval **(b)** logging period.

2 How can data be collected from sensors a long way from the computer?

Check the facts

Application software is designed to carry out user-related tasks.

All application software is written in a **computer language**. Most application software used on personal computers is bought as a ready-made package. The main types of package are summarised in the table below.

Applications

Type of package	Main uses
Word processing	Allows text to be entered, edited, formatted
Desktop publishing (DTP)	Allows text and graphics to be imported, positioned on a page, formatted, saved and printed
Database management system	Managing database files, designing queries, reports and forms
Spreadsheet	To hold data and formulae and carry out calculations and 'what if' investigations
Charting and graphing	To construct, save and print charts and graphs from data supplied by the user
Drawing	Produces drawings based on objects; easy to edit and resize
Painting	Produces pictures based on individual pixel colours
Graphics manipulation	Allows graphics files to be edited, combined and subjected to special effects
Web design	To design and publish websites; allows the pages to be assembled and hyperlinks to be made

Be careful when answering questions about packages. You will get no marks for brand names.

Test yourself

1 What is application software?

2 What type of package would you choose for **(a)** working out the cost of making a meal **(b)** producing a school newsletter **(b)** writing a letter?

Check the facts

> **Application software can be** specially
> **written or** existing packages can be altered
> **to meet the requirements of the user.**

The simplest way of altering a package to meet user requirements is to make **configuration changes**. These are changes in settings that can be reversed. An example of a configuration change is when buttons on a toolbar are changed to make features easier to use.

Packages can be **customised** by writing or recording macros. This adds program code. Changes can be extensive and may alter the way in which a package works.

A new package can be **written in a programming language**. This takes a long time and costs more than the other options, so it is only done if there is no alternative.

Method	Advantages	Disadvantage
Package configuration	• Can be reversed • Little or no cost • Doesn't take long	• The range of changes is limited • Changes not permanent
Package customisation	• Can give extra features • All the features of the package can be used • User need not know anything about using the package	• Takes time • Testing is needed for new features • Some cost involved
Programmining new package	• Will meet user requirements exactly • Won't have unwanted features	• Takes time to develop and test the program • Will cost more

Test yourself

1 What is the difference between a configuration change and customisation?

2 In what circumstances would it be sensible to produce a new package?

Check the facts

A **word-processing package** is used to produce documents containing text. The package has features to make the production of the document as easy as possible.

School Disco
Saturday 7 May
7pm
In the gym
Ticket Price £1.50

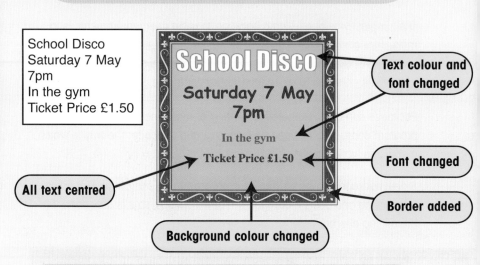

Text colour and font changed

Font changed

Border added

All text centred

Background colour changed

All word-processing packages allow the **font type** to be changed.

The **size and style of font** can also be altered.

Margins can be changed, and so can **line spacing**. **Justification** can be changed, so text can be **centred** or ranged right or left. The **colour of text** can also be changed.

Clip-art pictures can usually be added.

Most packages will allow **borders** to be put around the page or a paragraph. **Background colour** can often be changed.

Headers and footers can be used to add text to the top and bottom of every page.

Spell checkers help to avoid mistakes in the document.

Test yourself

1 Choose four features of a word-processing package and explain how each can be used to improve this notice:

> Lost
> Small brown dog with collar
> Contact Paul at 12 High Street if you find him

Applications

BBC GCSE Check and Test: ICT

51

Check the facts

A **desktop publishing package allows pages with a complex layout to be produced.** Text files and graphics **prepared elsewhere can be imported into the document.**

The package will allow **text and graphics frames** to be **created** and **positioned** on the page.

Text frames can be **linked** so that text automatically flows from one frame to the next.

The **background colour** and **border colour** of each frame can be changed.

Decorative heading

Picture frame with clip art picture

Text frame with border

Large **decorative headings** can be produced.

Styles can be created for **headings, sub-headings** and the **main body text.** These styles can be applied automatically.

Templates can be saved and used for **future publications.**

Test yourself

1 Explain how four different features of a desktop publishing package could be used to produce a page about a sports event for a school magazine.

2 Why might it be better to use a desktop publishing package for the task above, rather than a word-processing package?

Check the facts

A **drawing package produces** pictures made up of objects. The objects can all be handled separately, so the pictures are easy to edit.

This picture was produced using a drawing package.

Dots form the **drawing grid**. This helps to put objects in the correct place.

Some of the objects in this picture are clip-art images. They have been **imported** and **resized**.

The grass was drawn using a **special line** style. The grass is in the **front layer** of the picture.

The package has many other features, including:

 different fill styles for filling objects, such as boxes and stars

 a range of **pre-defined shapes** that can be drawn quickly

 a **large palette of colours** for lines and fills

 node-editing tools that allow objects to be adjusted after they have been drawn

 rotate-and-flip tools that allow objects to be twisted round or turned over

 text tools to allow text to be added to the picture.

All the **objects** in the picture can be **moved around separately**. They can be deleted if they are not needed and individual objects can be copied and pasted. The objects can be **grouped together**, so they can be handled as though they are one object.

Test yourself

1 Describe five features of a drawing package that you could use to produce a poster to advertise a school sports day.

2 What is the advantage of handling parts of a picture as separate objects?

Check the facts

Software packages designed for making web pages provide features not always found in word-processing and DTP packages. The page will have to be converted to a language called **Hypertext Markup Language** (HTML). The web-design software will be able to handle this conversion.

The GCSE Bitesize website uses most of the features of web-design software.

Web pages have text, graphics, animation, video clips and sound. The web-page design package will allow all of these things to be added. Text can be formatted and decorative styles can be used.

Applications

Web pages usually have some kind of **background**, so the package will **allow a choice of colours and effects**.

Web pages have **hyperlinks** to other pages. The software will allow creation of **text and graphics hyperlinks**. **Hotspots** can also be created. These are places on the page that act as links.

The software will allow the page to be **previewed in a web browser**, so appearance can be checked and hyperlinks tested.

Web-design software should also make it easy to **transfer the final web-page files** to the host computer belonging to the Internet Service Provider.

BBC GCSE Check and Test: ICT

Test yourself

1 Name four features that you would expect to find in a web-design package.

2 What language is used for web pages?

Applications

Check the facts

A spreadsheet package **is used to** carry out calculations **and to** investigate what happens if data changes.

Spreadsheets are made up of **cells**. Each cell has an **address** made up of the **column letter** and the **row number**. Cell B8 is in column B and row 8.

Cells in column A all contain text

Currency format used for prices

Cell B8

	A	B	C	D	E
	Item	Unit cost	Number of units needed	Item cost	
2	fabric	£ 6.50	0.25	£ 1.63	
3	eyes	£ 0.12	2	£ 0.24	
4	stuffing	£ 3.50	0.1	£ 0.35	
5	collar	£ 0.30	1	£ 0.30	
6	lead	£ 0.25	1	£ 0.25	
7					
8			Total cost of toy dog	£ 2.77	
9					
10					

Spreadsheets can hold **data or formulae**. Numbers can be in **different formats**.

A formula tells the spreadsheet to **carry out a calculation**. Cell D2 contains the formula = B2*C2. This tells the spreadsheet to **multiply** the value in B2 by the value in C2. The **answer** appears in cell D2.

All formulae start with =. If this is missed out, they won't work.

Spreadsheets have **functions**. The **SUM** function adds up all the cells in a range. Cell D8 uses SUM. The formula is = **SUM(D2:D6)**.

Test yourself

1 What is the address of the cell containing the item cost of stuffing?

2 Cell D5 contains a formula. Write down this formula.

3 The spreadsheet should work out the profit made if the toy is sold for £5.25.

   a) What changes would you need to make to the spreadsheet?

   b) Write a formula to work out the profit.

Check the facts

> **Spreadsheets are more useful than a calculator for many purposes.**

Spreadsheet

The spreadsheet can be more useful than a calculator because:

- it can be **saved and reused**
- **headings** can be used, so numbers make sense
- all the **intermediate steps** in the calculation can be seen
- the spreadsheet can be **printed out**
- **data can be changed** and the spreadsheet will **automatically produce the new answers**
- a spreadsheet can be **sent by e-mail** to another person
- the data in the spreadsheet can be used to **produce graphs and charts**.

	H	I	J	K	L
1					
2					
3	TOTAL	UNIT	Artwork	Author	Invest
4	revenue	REV			
5					
6					
7	4990	4.99	500	840	350
8	4990	4.99	500	720	350
9	9980	4.99	500	600	1500
10	2495	4.99	500	800	350
11	4990	4.99	200	640	500
12	7485	4.99	500	640	325
13	2495	4.99	500	800	350
14					
15					

Calculator

The calculator is more useful than the spreadsheet when:

- the calculation **only has to be done once**
- **only the final answer is needed** – there is no need to have headings or show intermediate answers
- there is **no computer** available
- **the person** doing the calculation **doesn't know how to use** the spreadsheet package.

Test yourself

1 A headteacher is working out how to spend money given to the school for sports equipment.

a) Give three reasons why a spreadsheet would be useful for this task.

b) Give two reasons why the headteacher may decide not to use a spreadsheet.

Check the facts

Applications

> Modelling software allows the user to carry out 'What if?' investigations. **Spreadsheets are often used to build models. Some of these models are complex.**

A model has **rules** and **variables**.

In a spreadsheet model:

- the **rules** are the **formulae**

- the **variables** are the **data values** used to work out the answer.

If these data values are changed, the answer will change. **Changing the formulae** will change the rules for the model. It will also change the answer.

When a model is built, it is important to ensure that the **rules are correct**. In complex models, there are many rules. If any are wrong, the answer will be wrong.

Computer models can be used to investigate long-term effects of change and to predict what will happen in the future. Predictions about the effects of climate change are made in this way.

Answers from computer models are not facts. They are **predictions** based on **rules** and **available data**.

Test yourself

1 Identify two variables that could be changed in this spreadsheet.

2 The toy dog is packed in a cardboard kennel costing 25 pence. The cost of this is to be built into the model.

   a) How would you add the cost of the kennel to the spreadsheet?

   b) Which existing formula would you have to change?

3 What limitations do computer models have?

	A	B	C	D	E
1	**Item**	**Unit cost**	**Number of units needed**	**Item cost**	
2	fabric	£ 6.50	0.25	£ 1.63	
3	eyes	£ 0.12	2	£ 0.24	
4	stuffing	£ 3.50	0.1	£ 0.35	
5	collar	£ 0.30	1	£ 0.30	
6	lead	£ 0.25	1	£ 0.25	
7					
8			**Total cost of toy dog**	£ 2.77	
9					
10			**Selling Price**	£ 5.25	
11					
12			**Profit**	£ 2.49	
13					
14					

Check the facts

Graphing software **and** charting software **allow graphs and charts to be produced from tables of data. The software may be part of a spreadsheet package or it may be a separate application.**

Graphing software

Graphing software can produce more types of graphs than simple charting software. It can plot graphs for mathematical expressions.

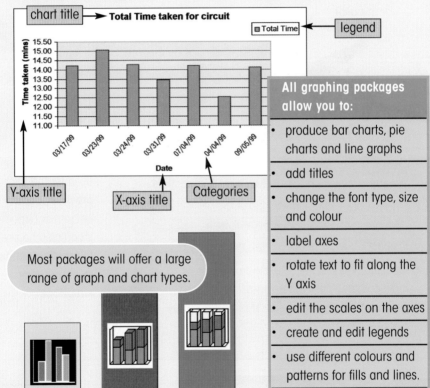

chart title → **Total Time taken for circuit**

legend

Y-axis title

X-axis title

Categories

Most packages will offer a large range of graph and chart types.

All graphing packages allow you to:

- produce bar charts, pie charts and line graphs
- add titles
- change the font type, size and colour
- label axes
- rotate text to fit along the Y axis
- edit the scales on the axes
- create and edit legends
- use different colours and patterns for fills and lines.

Applications

Test yourself

1 You have been asked to produce a chart to show the types of pets owned by pupils in your year group.

a) What type of chart would you make?

b) What features of the charting package would you use to create this chart?

BBC GCSE Check and Test: ICT

Check the facts

Simulation software **allows the user to create a computer** simulation model. **To simulate situations realistically, the model must be able to react quickly to inputs.**

Flight simulators are used to train pilots. The pilot has a set of controls the same as in an aeroplane.

- **The inputs** to the system are the adjustments that the pilot makes.
- **The outputs** change the position of the simulator and the graphics seen by the pilot

Simulators are used because:

✔ Simulation is cheaper than the real activity.

✔ Simulation is safer than the real activity.

✔ Simulation can be done repeatedly.

✔ Simulation takes less time than the real activity.

The limitations are:

✗ The rules are very complex and may not all apply in every situation.

✗ Some variables that affect the results may not be included in the model.

✗ A simulator is not the real thing and human reactions may not be the same. The pilot in the simulator knows he can't be hurt and this may alter his response.

The simulator can be used for the pilot to **practise landing** at unfamiliar airports. It can also be used to **practise actions in emergency situations**.

Test yourself

1 Give three reasons why simulators are used to train pilots.

2 Give two limitations of simulators.

Check the facts

> Data is stored in files. Within each file, data is divided into records. The records are all structured in the same way. They are divided into fields.

A **file** contains **data about one topic** (e.g. customers of a mail order company).

A **record** in the customer file contains **all the data about one customer**.

Fields have **names**. A field contains **one item of information** (e.g. surname).

Field name

Customer number	Title	Surname	Address	Town	Postcode
0001	Mr	Smith	12 High Street	Midtown	MD56 5AB
0002	Mrs	Patel	23 Percy Road	Craydon	CR4 12BY
0003	Mr	Raymond	45 Hillside Road	Bealdrey	CR6 8NC
0004	Ms	Close	127 Foley Drive	Midtown	MD27 5TN
0005	Mr	Manners	566 Main Road	Craydon	CR3 7GD

File   Field contents   Record

One field in each record is the **primary key field**. This field contains a value that doesn't occur in any other record in the file. This field **uniquely identifies the record** and makes finding records much easier.

Test yourself

1 Explain the terms 'file', 'record' and 'field'.

2 What is a 'primary key field'?

3 A file contains data about pupils. The pupils' surnames and forenames are two of the fields. Suggest two other fields that would be needed if a list of names of boys in form 7C were to be produced.

Check the facts

> The **fields** in a database **have their type defined when the database is created. This field type controls the type of data that can be entered.**

- A **text field** can contain any characters that can be typed in. It is not confined to letters.
- Text fields are given a **maximum length.** The length must be long enough for the data that will be entered.
- **Numeric fields**, or **number fields**, hold numbers. Calculations can be done with their contents.
- **True/False fields** can hold either true or false (Y or N) values.
- **Date/time fields** hold **dates and times.** Comparisons between dates can be made.

Record design

A **record design** is a list of all the fields in a record, with their types and lengths. The **primary key field** (area below shaded blue) should be identified.

Field name	Field type	Field length
Customer number	**Number**	**Automatic**
Title	text	4
Surname	text	18
Address	text	25
Town	text	14
Postcode	text	7

Applications

Test yourself

1 Give four different field types, with examples of data that could be stored.

2 A phone number is held in a text field instead of a numeric field. Why is this less likely to produce errors in data entry?

3 A pupil record contains fields for surname, forename, school year, form and gender. What field type and length would be best for each field?

www.bbc.co.uk/revision

Check the facts

> A **fixed-length record** consists of fixed-length fields. It is always the same size.
> **Variable-length records** change size depending on the data.

Fixed-length fields

The **surname field** is twelve characters long. This is how two different names are stored:

B	R	O	W	N							

H	A	R	R	I	N	G	T	O	N		

Both names use the same storage space. The empty part is filled with the character code for a space.

Fixed-length records are used so that a record will fit in the same space after editing. If a record is deleted, then another will fit in the same space. It is easy to work out the position of records in a database set up in this way.

Variable-length fields

End-of-field markers

B	R	O	W	N	

H	A	R	R	I	N	G	T	O	N	

Variable-length fields are the right length for each data item. An end-of-field marker is used to show where one field ends and the next begins.

Variable-length fields save storage space, but they make file-handling slower.

Test yourself

1 The following names are to be stored in a file:

George Elizabeth Vijay Margaret Reshma

How much space would be needed if:

a) a fixed-length field of ten characters were used?

b) a variable-length field were used, with commas as end-of-field markers?

Applications

BBC GCSE Check and Test: ICT

Check the facts

In a database, data is often organised into more than one file. The records in the files can be linked together using matching fields.

The library system below has three files:

Book File	Loan file	Member file
book number ··········	book number	member number
title	member number ····	title
author	date borrowed	forename
publisher		surname
ISBN		street
dewey code		town
		postcode

The member number in the **Loan file** matches a member number in the **Member file**. The book number in the **Loan file** matches a book number in the **Book file**.

Linking files **makes a database more flexible.**

Depending on where you start, lots of **information** can be extracted from one or more of the files using a query.

Organising files in this way **saves duplicating data**. If there was one file, the only way to store details of who borrowed the book would be in the **Book file**. The data would have to be added every time a member borrowed a book, and then deleted when the book was returned.

Test yourself

1 Give two advantages of using linked files rather than a single file for a library system.

2 Explain why a mailing-list system, used only to send letters to all members of a club, uses a single file.

Check the facts

We can make different comparisons between the field contents and the search value, depending on what we want to find out. Some comparisons only work with certain field types.

This table shows the type of comparisons that we can make.

Type of comparison	Applies to field types	Result of query
Equal to (=)	All	Finds records where the **field value** matches the search value **exactly**
Like	Text fields	Finds records where the field value is **like the given pattern** (e.g. Cl finds records where the search field value starts with Cl)
Greater than (>)	Numeric, text and date/time fields	Finds records with a field value **greater than** the **search value**
Less than (<)	Numeric, text and date/time fields	Finds records with a field value **less than** the **search value**
False	True/False fields	Finds records with a field value of **false**
True	True/False fields	Finds records with field value of **true**

Test yourself

1 What comparison would you use to find all the pupils in a school's database who were born after 31/08/88?

2 What comparison would you use to find all the pupils whose surname begins with 'D'?

Applications

BBC GCSE Check and Test: ICT

Check the facts

A database query is used to select required records from files in a database.

The query can **extract data** by comparing the contents of one or more fields with the value needed.

A simple query can be based on just **one field** and **one search value**.

Customer number	Title	Surname	Address	Town	Postcode
0001	Mr	Smith	12 High Street	Midtown	MD56 5AB
0002	Mrs	Patel	23 Percy Road	Craydon	CR4 12BY
0003	Mr	Raymond	45 Hillside Road	Bealdrey	CR6 8NC
0004	Ms	Close	127 Foley Drive	Midtown	MD27 5TN
0005	Mr	Close	566 Main Road	Craydon	CR3 7GD

A query is arranged as **\<field name\> \<comparison\> \<search value\>**

Searching the file for **Surname equal to 'Smith'** will find customer number 0001.

Searching the file for **Town equal to 'Craydon'** will find records for customer numbers 0002 and 0005.

Once the records have been found, they can be **printed** and the query **saved**, so the records can be found again.

Queries can also be used to **delete selected records** or to **make changes to groups of records**.

Test yourself

1 Write down the pattern for a simple query.

2 Write a query to find the customers from Bealdrey.

Applications

Check the facts

Complex queries **can be made by combining simple queries. Queries can be combined using the operators** AND **and** OR.

Customer number	Title	Surname	Address	Town	Postcode
0001	Mr	Smith	12 High Street	Midtown	MD56 5AB
0002	Mrs	Patel	23 Percy Road	Craydon	CR4 12BY
0003	Mr	Raymond	45 Hillside Road	Bealdrey	CR6 8NC
0004	Ms	Close	127 Foley Drive	Midtown	MD27 5TN
0005	Mr	Close	566 Main Road	Craydon	CR3 7GD

AND

Using **AND** that that **selects the records** where **both of the comparisons are true.**

The complex query is arranged as:

> **<field name> <comparison> <search value> <OPERATOR>**
> **<field name> <comparison> <search value>**

Searching for **Surname equal to 'Close' AND Town equal to 'Midtown'** will select the record for customer number 0004, Ms Close. It will not select customer 0005, because Mr Close does not live in Midtown.

OR

Using **OR** makes a query that selects the records where **at least one of the comparisons is true.** Searching for **Surname equal to 'Close' OR Town equal to 'Midtown'** finds customers 0001, 0004 and 0005.

NOT

The **NOT** operator can be used to **reverse the results** of a query.

This is arranged as **NOT (<field name> <comparison> <search value>).**

NOT (Town equal to 'Craydon') finds customers 0001, 0003 and 0004.

Test yourself

1 Write down the pattern for a complex query.

2 What are the operators that can be used to link simple queries?

3 Write a query to find the customers who live in Craydon or Bealdrey.

Applications

Check the facts

You can use **more than one file (table)** in a query. You just choose the fields you need from the linked tables.

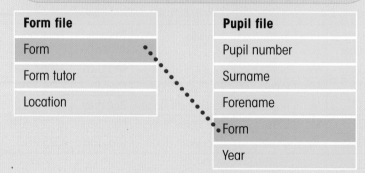

Form file
Form
Form tutor
Location

Pupil file
Pupil number
Surname
Forename
Form
Year

For example, you can find all the pupils in Form 7B and use the results of the query to print a list of surnames and forenames, with the name of the form tutor and location.

You start with the **Form file** and make a link to the **Pupil file** using the **form field**. You will need to include all the fields in the Form file and the surname and forename from the Pupil file in your query.

The query will need to find records with: **Form equal to '7B'**

The **database management system** will select the record for **Form 7B** in the Form file and each pupil record with **Form equal to '7B'** in the Pupil file.

Test yourself

1 A stock system has a suppliers file and a products file. The fields and link are shown below:

Supplier file
Supplier code
Supplier name
Address
Town
Postcode

Product file
Product number
Description
Supplier code
Number in stock

a) Write a query to find all products from the supplier with the code 17.

b) Write a query to find all the products from supplier number 17 where there are less than one hundred in stock.

Check the facts

A relational database management system is the software that allows a user to manage a database system efficiently. **It provides** tools **for setting up all parts of the database system.**

The window below shows part of a database management package. From the window, all parts of the database system can be created and used.

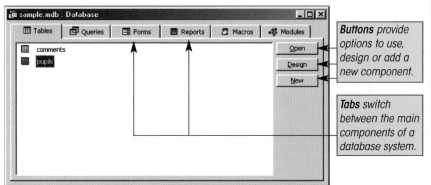

Buttons *provide options to use, design or add a new component.*

Tabs *switch between the main components of a database system.*

The **table section** lets the user design new file structures or open existing files to see the data.

The **query section** lets the user build and use new queries based on one or more tables.

The **forms section** is for producing and opening data-input forms.

The **reports section** is for creating and opening reports to be output to the printer or screen. A report gets its data from a table or a query.

All these components can be saved and used again. The management system makes it possible to build up complex database systems a little at a time.

Test yourself

1 Describe three tasks that you would expect to be able to do using a database management system.

Applications

BBC GCSE Check and Test: ICT

Check the facts

Mail-merge is a way of using fields from a data file to insert data into a word-processed document. **It is mostly used to personalise standard letters.**

The letter below is to be sent to every customer on the database. When the letter is printed, the data is inserted in place of the field names.

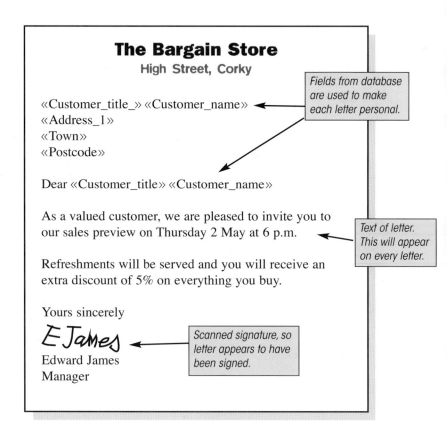

The Bargain Store
High Street, Corky

«Customer_title_» «Customer_name»
«Address_1»
«Town»
«Postcode»

Dear «Customer_title» «Customer_name»

As a valued customer, we are pleased to invite you to our sales preview on Thursday 2 May at 6 p.m.

Refreshments will be served and you will receive an extra discount of 5% on everything you buy.

Yours sincerely

E James

Edward James
Manager

Fields from database are used to make each letter personal.

Text of letter. This will appear on every letter.

Scanned signature, so letter appears to have been signed.

Mail-merging is mainly used in **advertising**, using mailing lists owned by an organisation or bought from another company.

Test yourself

1 Explain what is meant by 'mail-merging'.

2 Give one use of mail-merging.

Check the facts

> Batch processing **is a method used when all records need to be processed at the same time. This method can be used to process data held on a** serial medium, **such as** magnetic tape.

Processing does not take place until all data is available. Once a batch process has started, **it needs no human input**.

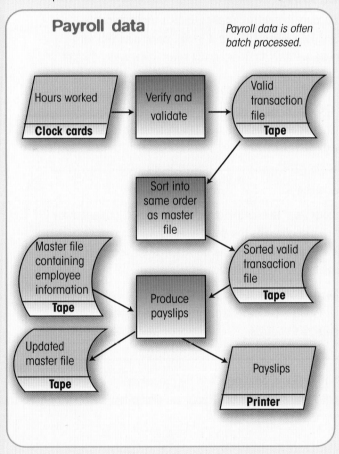

Payroll data

Payroll data is often batch processed.

- **Data is input** about hours worked by each employee.

- This data is **validated** and then **stored** in a transaction file.

- The transaction file is **sorted into the same order as the master file**.

- A **record** is now read from the master and transaction files.

- Pay is calculated and an **updated employee record** is written to a new copy of the master file.

- A **payslip** is printed.

Processing

BBC GCSE Check and Test: ICT

Test yourself

1 What is batch processing?

2 Describe the stages in a batch-processing application.

Check the facts

> **Real-time processing** happens when outputs are produced quickly enough to influence further inputs. **Transaction processing** occurs when each change is processed as it occurs.

Processing

Real-time processing

Real-time processing occurs in **control applications**, usually through **feedback systems**. Simulators, such as **flight simulators**, also use real-time processing. In these systems, time delays of even a few seconds are not acceptable.

transaction processing

Booking systems, on-line ordering systems and library loan systems are **transaction processed**.

Library loan system

When you borrow a book from the library, a **record** is created straight away in the **Loan file**. This record contains the book number, your member number and the date that you borrowed the book. Once the record has been created, the book is your responsibility.

When the book is brought back, the return is entered into the system straight away. This is important because it means that the book becomes available for someone else to borrow.

In transaction-processed systems, data needs to be processed quickly, but the timing is not critical. If the system is busy, you can wait a few seconds.

Test yourself

1 Explain the difference between a real-time system and a transaction-processed system.

2 Why is transaction processing used for library systems?

Check the facts

> Data files sometimes need to be sorted into a
> required order ready for processing.

Physically sorting a file means moving the records around to get them in the correct order. It is not the same as changing the index used to order records in a database file.

> Sorting is mostly done when data is held in
> serial access files.

The **transaction files** used in **batch processing** have to be sorted. Because the records are entered in the order in which they are received, they need to be rearranged in the same order as the records in the master file. This allows records from the two files to be matched during processing.

Master file order	Transaction file order
2001	2002
2002	2018
2003	2005
2004	2003
2005	2014
2006	2015
2007	2001
2008	2004
2009	2008
2010	2007

If the transaction file is not sorted, the records do not match up. Record 1 in the master file is matched to record 7 in the transaction file instead of record 1.

Test yourself

1 What is sorting of a data file?

2 Why is sorting sometimes necessary?

Check the facts

> **Merging files is combining files in a way that keeps all the records in the correct order.**

Files are merged when they come from **several sources** and **need to be combined for processing**. In some applications, data is entered by lots of different operators working on different computers. Each operator produces a file, sorted into order. All these separate files are combined to make one very large file.

During the merging process, records are read from the small files. They are compared and then written in the correct order to the new file.

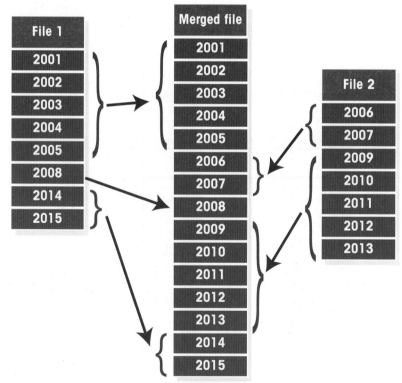

Test yourself

1 When is it necessary to merge files?

2 Explain how the records end up in the correct order.

Check the facts

Graphics files can be large and are often compressed. Compression is reducing the file size by changing the way in which the data is stored.

Compression can be applied to any file, but the effect will differ depending on the nature of the file.

One way of compressing a file is to **remove repeating values**. This can be done by saving the value and the number of times it is repeated. Graphics files can be compressed in this way.

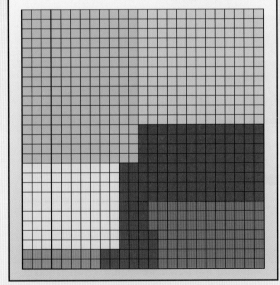

This bitmapped image has lots of repeats of coloured pixels. Compression would greatly reduce file size.

Database files can be compressed by **removing spaces from text fields**. Provided the number of spaces is stored in the compressed file, the database file can be restored to its original fixed field-length form when it is expanded.

Word-processed files can be compressed by **removing spaces and blank lines**.

Processing

Test yourself

1 What is file compression and why is it used?

2 How can a bitmapped graphics file be compressed?

Check the facts

> The cost of **storage media** has fallen considerably and most users don't worry too much about the size of files, although large files can present problems.

Large files can become a problem if they have to be transmitted as **e-mail attachments or put on a web page**. They take longer to transmit using communication links.

Lots of large graphics files can make a web page slow to load, so the user may give up and look at another website. **JPEG** and **GIF graphics files** are saved in a compressed form and therefore work better on web pages than bitmapped files. Sound and video files can also be large.

> If files have to be put on a **floppy disk**, they must be **smaller than 1.44 Mb.**

Large databases with thousands of records can take up a lot of space. Database records are often simply marked as 'deleted' when the user chooses to delete the record. **Packing the database** removes these records and releases the space.

Test yourself

1 Why do users no longer worry about file size?

2 Give three situations where file size can be a problem.

Processing

Check the facts

> Computer-controlled systems **range from relatively simple temperature-control systems to complex autopilot systems on aeroplanes.**

All these systems are **real-time systems**. This means that the system is fast enough for the outputs to affect further inputs.

The basic components of a control system are the **sensors** that detect the changes, the **devices** that are turned on and off, the **computer or microprocessor** and the **control program** that makes the system work.

A heating control system works as shown in the diagram below.

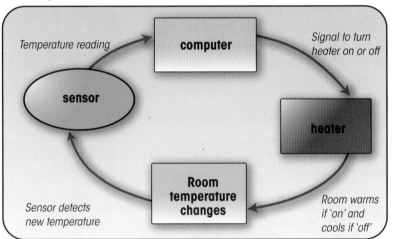

Temperature reading → **computer** → *Signal to turn heater on or off*

sensor

heater

Sensor detects new temperature

Room temperature changes

Room warms if 'on' and cools if 'off'

This is a **feedback system**, which keeps the temperature within set limits. The computer controlling the system is often a microprocessor. The program that controls the system works as shown opposite.

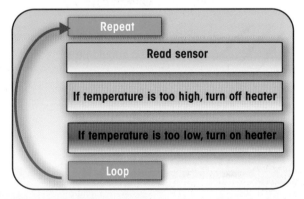

Repeat

Read sensor

If temperature is too high, turn off heater

If temperature is too low, turn on heater

Loop

Test yourself

1 What are the main components of a control system?

2 Control systems are real-time systems. Explain the meaning of 'real time'.

Processing

Check the facts

Data can be lost because of **physical damage** to the medium on which it is stored. The main threats are **heat, water, magnetic fields** and **dirt**.

HEAT: all storage media can be damaged by heat. **Fire prevention** is important and automatic alarm systems should be used.

WATER: storage media and whole computer systems can be damaged by water. **Flooding can cause serious damage**. If the risk of floods is high, computer equipment and media should be located in places not likely to get wet. Simple spills can cause damage, so keep drinks away from media and computers.

MAGNETIC FIELDS: the data on magnetic disks and tapes can be **corrupted by magnetic fields**. Power lines, phones, monitors and powerful motors all generate magnetic fields, so care must be taken when storing media.

DIRT: the media and drive can be damaged if there is **dirt on the disk or tape surface**. Disks and tapes should be stored in dust-proof containers.

SCRATCHES: optical media can be scratched or broken. CDs and DVDs should be **stored safely**.

Test yourself

1 Data on magnetic media can be damaged.

a) Describe three physical threats to this data.

b) Explain how these threats could be minimised.

2 How can data on an optical medium be damaged?

Check the facts

> Data loss or corruption **can occur because of accidental or deliberate damage. This can be caused by people authorised to work with the data or by people making unauthorised access.**

Accidental damage

Accidental damage happens when **users make mistakes**. This can happen if software packages are difficult to use or if staff have not been properly trained.

Deliberate damage

Deliberate damage to data can be done by **people with access to the system as part of their job**. Damage can be discouraged by keeping a log file of everyone who has used the data. This log can be used to work out who caused the damage.

Denying access to data that the user does not need limits opportunities to cause damage.

Deliberate damage can be done by **people who make unauthorised access to the system**. The risk can be reduced by:

- **using passwords** that are changed regularly, so they are less likely to be known to outsiders
- **locking user access** after a few wrong attempts to make it more difficult to break into the system by guessing
- **logging off** or **locking terminals** whenever they are left unattended.

Test yourself

1 Give two causes of accidental damage to data.

2 Give three ways of preventing unauthorised access to a system.

Security

BBC GCSE Check and Test: ICT

Check the facts

**A virus is a computer program that can replicate itself.
Some viruses are able to damage data.**

Viruses can be **spread** on **infected floppy disks**, as **e-mail attachments** and **through some web sites**.

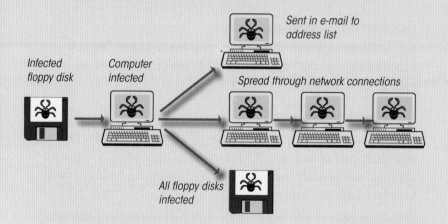

*Infected
floppy disk*

*Computer
infected*

*Sent in e-mail to
address list*

Spread through network connections

*All floppy disks
infected*

Once a virus has infected a computer, it may act in various ways. Some viruses are designed to send **infected e-mails** to all the addresses in the e-mail address book.

Viruses can **spread through open network connections**, so one infected e-mail could infect every computer on the network.

Many viruses damage data. They may change or delete vital system files so that software has to be re-installed. Some viruses **do not activate straight away**. They may be triggered by a date or a particular sequence of actions.

Virus-checking software

Virus-checking software prevents known viruses getting into a computer and will delete viruses from infected disks. The virus definitions need to be updated regularly, as new viruses appear all the time.

Test yourself

1 What is a virus? How does a virus spread?

2 How can a computer be protected from infection by viruses?

Security

www.bbc.co.uk/revision

Check the facts

Making backup copies of data is vital. If anything goes wrong with the computer system and data is lost, backup copies can be used to restore the lost or damaged files.

If processing is done every time a transaction occurs, the method of backup is usually a two-stage process.

1 File copies

Stage 1 is to **make a copy of all the data files**. This is done at least once a day, usually to tape.

2 Transaction logs

Stage 2 is **making a transaction log file**. This contains a copy of every transaction that occurs. Records are written to the log file as each transaction is processed.

The backup files must be on a **different storage medium** to the main files. There is no point having all the copies on one hard disk. It is best if the backup storage devices are in another building, or at least another room.

The backup media are **rotated**. This means that a different tape is used for each day of the week.

The file copies and transaction logs are **labelled and kept together in a fireproof store**. Both will be needed if the data has to be restored.

Test yourself

1 Describe the method of backup for transaction-processed files.

2 Why must the backup copies be separate from the working copies?

Security

Check the facts

> The files used in batch processing can be kept for backup purposes. It is normal to have three sets of files. The method is referred to as the file generation or the Grandfather, Father and Son system of backup.

Security

The Father

The **Father file** is the **master file** that was made during the previous batch process.

The Son

The **Son file** is the **new master file** that is created once batch processing is complete. If the new file is lost, a copy can be made by repeating the processing using the Father file and the transaction file.

The Grandfather

It is possible for the Father file to be damaged during processing, so the version before that is always kept. It is called the **Grandfather file**. It can be used with the **transaction file** to make a new copy of the Father file.

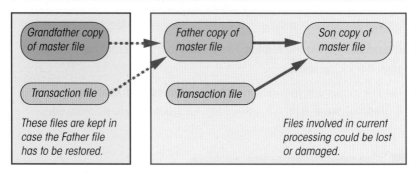

Grandfather copy of master file

Father copy of master file

Son copy of master file

Transaction file

Transaction file

These files are kept in case the Father file has to be restored.

Files involved in current processing could be lost or damaged.

This method ensures the working files can be restored. Media containing files older than the Grandfather file can be reused.

Test yourself

1 Explain why three versions of the master file are kept.

2 Why are the transaction files kept?

Check the facts

> **Network file servers** hold a huge number of files
> created by users. These files should be backed up regularly.
> The network servers will also have important system files.
> All this data must be backed up as well.

Network backups are made to **magnetic tape** held on small cassettes.
These tapes have a **very high capacity**. A full backup of the server drives is
usually made at intervals, perhaps once a week. In between these full
backups, **incremental backups** are made every day. These provide copies
of the files that have changed since the last full backup.

Magnetic tape backup

The tapes are organised
so they can be **reused regularly**.
The length of time for which a tape is kept before being reused depends on
how quickly lost data is likely to be discovered. If there are lots of users,
some files may not be used very often and problems may not be found for
a while.

If a user discovers that a file has been lost or damaged, the **backup
software allows a copy of that file to be restored**.

Test yourself

1 How often are backup copies of files on a network server made?

2 Why are tapes kept for a few days before being reused?

Security

BBC GCSE Check and Test: ICT

Check the facts

User identification codes are codes that have to be entered before logging onto a system. Passwords can prevent others using someone else's ID code. Levels of access control what individual users can do while logged onto the system.

User IDs are often built up in a **standard way** for all users. This makes it easy to identify a particular user, but it does mean other users can work out the codes.

Users can be given access to particular files or directories. Different levels of access are possible. This table shows how access levels can be used:

Level	Access allowed	Given to
Top level	Full access to all software and files	Network managers and database administrators
Middle level	Read and write access to some files	General users who only need access to their own work
Low level	Read access to some files	Staff who do not need to change data but do need to see it
No access	No access to any files	Staff who do not need to use the computer systems

Passwords should be **changed regularly**. Users should not be allowed to choose passwords that are easy to guess. **Password hierarchies** can be used, so users need special passwords to use particular files.

 ## Test yourself

1 How do access levels help to keep a system secure?

2 Why should users not be able to choose their own passwords?

Check the facts

> **Encrypting data is changing the data so it can't be understood if it is stolen.**

Data can be **encrypted** when it is stored. This means that if **someone makes a copy of the data, it won't make any sense** when he or she opens the file. Getting the data back into its original form requires knowledge of the way in which the data was encrypted.

Data can also be encrypted when it is **transmitted** from one computer to another. This is a point at which **data can be intercepted**, so it makes sense to encrypt anything confidential.

Encryption is always a **complex pattern of alteration**. The example below shows how it works.

> **This is the message**

> Add 16 to the ASCII code of each character we get

> dxy|Oy|O|xuO}u||qwu

> This version doesn't make much sense.

Strong encryption is used to protect sensitive data such as **credit card numbers**, when they are transmitted through the Internet to pay for items bought on-line.

Security

Test yourself

1 What is encryption?

2 Explain why encryption is necessary when data is transmitted from one computer to another.

BBC GCSE Check and Test: ICT

Networks and communication

Check the facts

The computers in a Local Area Network (LAN) are connected together by cables. The network is in a single building or small area. There are different ways in which the connections can be arranged. These are called network topologies.

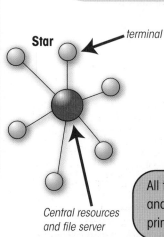

Star — terminal

Central resources and file server

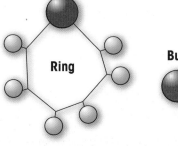

Ring

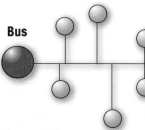

Bus

All the computers (terminals) in a LAN can **communicate** and **share the central resources**, such as hard disks, printers, application software and data files.

Advantages

✔ If applications and user files are kept on the file server, they can be used on any terminal.

✔ Central backup can be carried out.

✔ Security can be controlled centrally.

✔ Printers can be shared.

Disadvantages

✘ If there is a problem with the file server, none of the terminals will be able to use the central resources.

✘ If a network cable fails, at least one terminal will be unable to use central resources.

✘ A virus on one terminal can spread through a network.

Test yourself

1 Give three advantages of having a network rather than the same number of stand-alone computers.

2 Name the three main network topologies.

Check the facts

A Wide Area Network (WAN) is connected by communication links, not network cables. The network can cover a wide area. The largest WAN is the Internet, which is a global network.

Large organisations with many branches often have their own **WAN**.

The communication lines used can be **ordinary phone lines, ISDN lines** and **broadband connections**.

If a standard phone line is used, the **computers at both ends** of the connection **must have modems**.

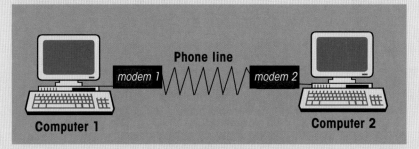

- **Modem 1** converts the **digital signal** from computer A to an **analogue signal** that can travel along the phone line.
- **Modem 2** converts the **analogue signal** back to **digital form** and passes it to computer B.

ISDN line

An ISDN line gives a **much faster connection** than a modem, but it does **cost more**. Because several channels can be used, it is a good choice if several computers share the same WAN connection.

Broadband

Broadband provides **more bandwidth** than an ordinary phone line, so **communication is faster**. It can carry **voice and data at the same time**.

Test yourself

1 Why is a modem necessary if a telephone line is used for a wide area connection?

2 Arrange the following in descending order of speed-of-data transfer:
(a) phone line **(b)** ISDN **(c)** broadband.

Networks and communication

BBC GCSE Check and Test: ICT

Check the facts

E-mail provides a rapid way of sending messages and data files to specific addresses anywhere in the world.

To send e-mail, you need to have an **e-mail address**. This provides a **mailbox** on a **mail server**. You must also know the e-mail address of the person to whom you are sending the e-mail. The process works like this:

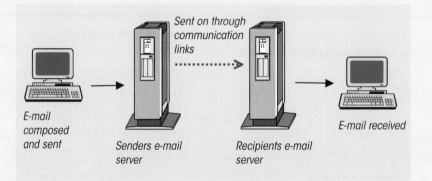

E-mail composed and sent

Senders e-mail server

Sent on through communication links

Recipients e-mail server

E-mail received

Files can be attached to an e-mail. The file can be opened and saved separately by the person who receives the e-mail.

Any kind of file can be attached. **Pictures**, **documents**, **database files** and **computer programs** can all be sent in this way.

The same e-mail can be sent to a whole **list of people** at the **same time**.

E-mail accounts are **password protected**, so an e-mail should reach the person to whom it is addressed.

The e-mail stays on the **mail server** until it is retrieved. E-mails can be collected the next time the recipient turns on his or her computer.

Test yourself

1 What happens when an e-mail is sent?

2 Name three kinds of file that can be sent with an e-mail.

Check the facts

E-mail is one method of communicating; there are other methods available.

	e-mail	Phone	Fax	Post
Speed	Almost instant	Instant	About 30 seconds to connect, plus transmission time, depending on length of document	24 hours or more, depending on destination
Security	Good, goes to a specified e-mail address	Good, the person has to answer the call	Can be read by anyone at fax machine location	Can be opened by anyone at postal address
Range of data	Any kind of file can be attached	Voice only	Text and graphics	Anything that can be put in an envelope or parcel
Cost	Local phone call, regardless of destination	Depends on destination and length of transmission	Depends on destination and length of transmission	Depends on weight and destination; costs more than any other method
Multiple copies	Yes	Needs conference-call facility	Each copy requires a separate phone call	Have to be sent separately
Needs recipient present	No	Yes, but messages can be left	No	No

Test yourself

1 Give three advantages of using e-mail rather than post to send a picture of yourself to a relative in another country.

2 Give an example of a situation where communication by post would be necessary.

3 Give three reasons why e-mail would be the best method of sending a fifty-page report to ten people in different parts of the country.

Networks and communication

BBC GCSE Check and Test: ICT

Networks and communication

Check the facts

The **Internet** is a **Global Wide Area Network.**
Servers on the Internet hold vast amounts of data. The
Internet is not located in one place; it is a worldwide
collection of computers, which all have Internet
connections provided by communication links.

The **World Wide Web** is
the best known part of the
Internet. It is a **collection
of websites**.

Every website has an **address**
called a **Uniform Resource
Locator**, or **URL**. The full URL starts
with **http://**, but web browsers
always add this part at the beginning.

Websites can be **produced by
anyone**, so care is needed when
deciding how reliable the source
of information is likely to be.

Chat rooms and **Usenet
newsgroups** are also part of the
Internet. They allow people with
particular interests to communicate.

Always remember that people do
not have to give their true identities
in chat rooms and Usenet
newsgroups and they may not be
who they seem to be.

**Never tell anyone in a chat
room your name, address or
phone number. Never arrange
to meet anyone you have met
on the Internet.**

www.bbc.co.uk/revision

Test yourself

1 What is the World Wide Web?

2 How are websites identified?

Check the facts

> **A web browser is used to find websites on the Internet. The browser can download the files that make up the web page. It uses the HTML instructions to display the page on the screen.**

Web browsers store the **history of sites visited** during a day or longer. This makes it easy to go back to places that you have been to before. The browser can keep a list of **favourite sites**. This is useful when sites are very big and you frequently want to get to the same place.

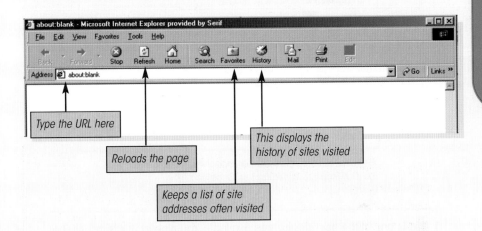

Type the URL here

Reloads the page

This displays the history of sites visited

Keeps a list of site addresses often visited

The image above shows one of the browsers available. The **address line** is where you **type the URL** of the site you want to visit. If you don't know the address, you can use one of the **search engines** to find it.

Test yourself

1 What is a web browser?

2 Describe three useful features of a web browser.

Networks and communication

BBC GCSE Check and Test: ICT

Check the facts

The Internet is enormous and finding the right site can be difficult. There are special sites with **search facilities** to help find sites of interest. The **search engine** asks for a word or words for the search.

Type your word here

An advanced search option is available

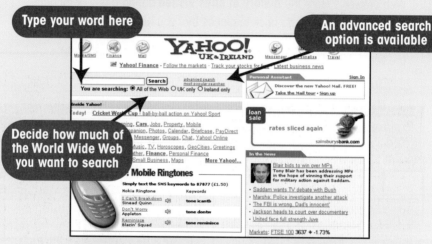

Decide how much of the World Wide Web you want to search

Reproduced with permission of Yahoo! Inc. YAHOO! and the YAHOO! logo are trademarks of Yahoo! inc.

This is one of the **search engines** available. You type in words or use the **advanced search options** to narrow down your search.

When the search is complete, a **list of websites** is displayed. If there are too many sites, you can change your search criteria. The list is **in order of probable relevance**, so you should find what you want quite quickly.

Test yourself

1 Give two reasons why you might want to use a search engine to find information on the Internet.

2 When would you use an advanced search?

3 This search engine lets you choose how much of the web to include in the search. Give one advantage of limiting the search to one country.

Networks and communication

Check the facts

E-commerce is **trading through the Internet. Most major retailers have websites and sell** on-line. **You can buy everything from groceries to a new car or a holiday on the web. Banking is also available** on-line. **Airline and train tickets can be booked** on-line.

On-line trading has **advantages** and **disadvantages**, which include:

Advantages

✔ **A range of products and suppliers** can be checked before buying.

✔ **There are** no sales staff selling you products that you don't really want.

✔ **You** don't need to travel to the shops.

✔ **There are often** discounts for on-line purchases.

✔ **You can** usually find what you want **somewhere on the web.**

Disadvantages

✗ **You can see pictures of what you are buying, but you can't handle anything.**

✗ **You may have to** pay for delivery.

✗ **There is** no social contact.

✗ **Buying from** unknown suppliers may be risky – the goods may not arrive.

✗ **You can't ask questions about products before you buy them.**

On-line banking

On-line banking is fast and easy. Money can be transferred from one account to another and bank statements can be seen. Banking is secure, but some people still think security risks outweigh advantages.

Test yourself

1 What is e-commerce?

2 Give three different examples of on-line trading.

3 Give two advantages and two disadvantages of buying groceries on-line.

Networks and communication

BBC GCSE Check and Test: ICT

Check the facts

On-line booking is available for trains, flights, holidays, sporting events, concerts and the theatre. Booking is easy and you know straight away whether the tickets you want are available.

book online   step 12345

To check availability and fares, simply tell us where you want to fly and when. Your choice of routes now includes all those operated by Go. All Go flights are now fully integrated into this booking system. The terms and conditions that apply to flights previously booked through go-fly.com are available here.

from	to
Aberdeen (ABZ)	Aberdeen (ABZ)
Amsterdam (AMS)	Amsterdam (AMS)
Athens (ATH)	Athens (ATH)
Alicante (ALC)	Alicante (ALC)

flying out on   returning on
26 ◆ February 2003 ◆   no, ◆ just one way   ◆

no. of passengers
adults 0 ◆ children 0 ◆ infants 0 ◆
               (2 to 13 years)   (under 2 years)

show prices   Please read these important notes before booking.

The image above shows an on-line flight booking system. The system collects information on where the customer wants to go and the travel dates. It will then show available flights and prices for these dates.

Once the customer has filled in all the sections of the booking form, the **data is transmitted** to the company. The seat on the flight is booked and **confirmation is sent by e-mail**.

All of this happens automatically. The booking system is **cheap to run** and **prices are low**. The company still makes a profit, because **few staff** are needed to operate this system.

The system **changes the price** as the number of seats available falls. If there are lots of seats available, the seats are very cheap; if there are few seats available, the cost rises.

Test yourself

1 What are the advantages of an on-line booking system for
(a) the customers **(b)** the company?

Check the facts

Devices such as digital televisions, mobile phones and digital cameras and software such as web browsers are becoming integrated, so they can all be used for communication.

Digital television is interactive. Using phone lines, **e-mail messages** can be sent from a TV set. **On-line purchasing** is also available from digital TV sets.

Mobile phones can include **digital cameras**. The resulting pictures can be sent by e-mail anywhere in the world. Internet access is possible from some mobile phones, although it is still too expensive to be widely used.

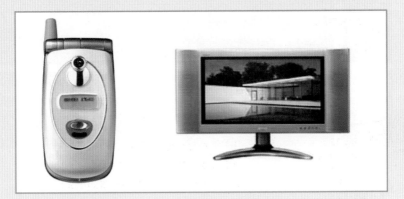

These developments remove the need for a computer to send e-mails. Communication is possible **even in remote areas**.

Integration is moving quickly, and we can expect that integrated devices will become easier to use and will offer more and more services.

Test yourself

1 What benefits are available from integration of communication devices?

Check the facts

> The increasing use of ICT has had many effects on the way in which we work. Some traditional jobs **have almost disappeared**, while new skills **have become necessary.**

The increasing use of ICT has affected most jobs, because they now involve some use of computers.

Check-out operators in supermarkets use bar-code scanners and don't have to be able to add up prices or work out change.

Office staff use word processors and there are **fewer paper records to be filed**.

There has been an increase in **working from home**. Remote access to company systems **makes this much easier**. Work can also be moved **between home and office by e-mail**.

National boundaries are becoming easier to ignore. Many **call centres are located abroad**, because **phone calls can be easily transferred to other countries**. Pay is lower in these areas and access to the data needed to answer the questions that customers ask is instantly available.

New jobs for those with technical skills have been created. Systems analysts, programmers, network management staff, website designers and hardware experts are all in demand.

Test yourself

1 Give four ways in which jobs have changed with the increased use of ICT.

2 Why is working from home easier when ICT is used?

Check the facts

In education, on-line resources and interactive whiteboards have changed the way in which many subjects are taught. For pupils, there is more emphasis on researching topics and producing presentations.

The **Internet** is an important resouce for pupils. It is becoming the **first place to look** when information is needed. The results of the research may be organised into a **multimedia presentation** or presented as a **colourful, word-processed report**.

E-mail can be used to communicate with pupils in other schools, and sometimes **in other countries**. This can widen understanding of languages, cultural differences and lifestyles.

Pupil records are almost always **held on computer systems**. This can make it **much easier to track pupil performance** and identify **problem areas** so that help can be given.

In higher education, applications can be made electronically and the **progress of each individual application can be checked** on the Internet. Students find that **all work must be word-processed**. Assignments are **submitted by e-mail** and lecture notes may be available on the Internet.

Test yourself

1 Describe three ways in which ICT has changed the way in which pupils work.

2 What are the advantages of using the Internet when carrying out a project on earthquakes for geography?

ICT and society

BBC GCSE Check and Test: ICT

Check the facts

ICT has affected the social life and leisure activities of many people. While some of these effects have been positive, others have been negative.

Computer games are an important **leisure activity** for many people. Games are a **good way to relax**, but they are sometimes used for many hours. This type of activity **restricts social contact**.

ICT is used within the leisure industry. **Modern theme parks** make extensive use of ICT systems to control rides. Some rides are **computer simulations**.

Many **films** have been made using **ICT to produce special effects**. Several characters have been **computer generated**.

Modern **communication systems** make it possible to **watch sporting events from around the world**.

Concerts and other events are **shown live on the Internet**.

ICT may have resulted in some people staying at home more, but it has also made a **great contribution to the entertainment industry**.

ICT has caused **problems for the producers of music CDs**, as these can **easily be copied**.

Test yourself

1 Describe three different ways in which ICT has helped the leisure industry.

2 Describe one way in which ICT may have a damaging effect on the entertainment industry.

3 Describe one way in which leisure use of ICT can have a negative effect on people.

Check the facts

> Data needs to be accurate. There should be procedures in place to make sure the accuracy of data is regularly checked. If data is not accurate, the effects can be serious.

One inaccuracy that is quite common is for records not to be updated after a **person has moved house**. This often results in **junk mail** being delivered to the previous address. More seriously, if the person had a **bad credit rating**, the **new occupants** may be **refused credit** on the basis of their **postcode**.

If medical records are inaccurate, the results **can be disastrous**. Someone with an allergy, for example, could die if he or she receives the wrong treatment.

Why do inaccuracies occur?

Inaccuracies can occur for various reasons:

- Data may **not have been collected**.
- Data could **be wrong** because the person gave wrong information.
- Sometimes there are **mistakes in data entry**.
- Records can be **deleted accidentally**.

Mistakes in data entry are usually responsible for situations where customers get **huge bills for utilities**, such as electricity.

Test yourself

1 Give three ways in which inaccuracies in data can arise.

2 Describe three possible effects of inaccuracies in data.

ICT and society

BBC GCSE Check and Test: ICT

Copyright law and licensing

Check the facts

Software Piracy

It is illegal to make extra copies of software, **except for backup purposes**. Likewise, it is illegal to buy one copy of a package and then install it on more than one computer.

Making or installing **extra copies** of software is called **software piracy** and is a **crime**. If an organisation needs more copies of a package, it can **buy extra licences.**

Legal aspects

There are different kinds of licence:

1 A **single-user** licence allows the software to be installed and used **on one computer**.

single-user

2 A **multi-user** licence allows the package to be installed and used on a **stated number of computers**.

multi-user

3 A **site licence** allows the software to be installed and used on **any number of computers**, provided they are **all on one site**. A site is usually one building or a group of linked buildings.

site licence

Software is sometimes provided free of charge by the copyright owner. It is still covered by the copyright law, but permission is given to make copies and give them away.

Test yourself

1 What is software piracy?

2 Mr Brown has bought an item of software to use on his computer. He wants to use the same package on his notebook computer. Why can't he just install the package on this computer as well?

Check the facts

> The Computer Misuse Act of 1990
> deals with hacking. Hacking is gaining
> unauthorised access to a computer system.
> The person who does this is called a hacker.
> Some hackers break into systems to show
> they can beat the security, while others
> intend to damage data or programs.

There are **three levels of offence** under this act:

1 Making **unauthorised access** to computer **programs or data**. Accessing a system and looking at the data when you have no right to do so is a crime.

2 Making **unauthorised access** with the **intention to commit a further crime** is a more serious offence. It covers activities such as trying to steal data.

3 Making **unauthorised modifications to programs or data** covers any damage caused by people not authorised to use the system. **Deliberately spreading computer viruses** or breaking into a system and **deleting or altering data** are offences under this section of the act.

Hackers can break into the system from outside. People who work for an organisation can also commit offences under the act.

Test yourself

1 What is hacking?

2 What are the three levels of offence under the Computer Misuse Act?

Legal aspects

BBC GCSE Check and Test: ICT

Check the facts

> The Data Protection Act of 1998 controls the way in which personal data about living people can be collected and used. The act applies to all personal data, whether or not it is in a computer-readable format.

Personal data is divided into two types: **ordinary data** and **sensitive data**.

Ordinary data

Ordinary personal data includes name, address, date of birth and details of items bought and payments made.

Sensitive data

Sensitive data is data about racial or ethnic origin, religious beliefs, political views, health, criminal records, sexual preferences and trade union membership. There are **extra rules** about how **sensitive data** is collected and used.

Any organisation holding personal data must **notify the Data Protection Commission** about what data they hold. They must state what they use the data for, where they get the data from and to whom the data may be passed.

Data users must obey the **eight data protection principles**.

Data subjects are given **seven rights** by the act.

There are some types of data that are **exempt from all or part of the act**.

Test yourself

1 What must organisations holding personal data tell the Data Protection Commission?

2 Give three examples of sensitive personal data.

3 What is the purpose of the Data Protection Act?

Legal aspects

www.bbc.co.uk/revision

Check the facts

There are **eight data protection principles.** These control how data users collect and use **personal data.** Organisations must appoint a **data controller** to make sure that the principles are obeyed.

1 Personal data must be collected and **processed fairly and lawfully.** It can only be processed if certain conditions are met.

2 Personal data must be obtained for **specific purposes** and can't be used for other purposes.

3 Personal data must be **adequate, relevant** and **not excessive** for the purpose for which it is obtained.

4 Personal data must be **accurate** and must be kept **up to date.**

5 Personal data must **not be kept for longer than necessary.** It must be deleted or destroyed when it is no longer needed.

6 Personal data must be processed **with regard to the rights of the data subject.**

7 Personal data must be **kept safe and secure** from accidental or deliberate damage.

8 Personal data **cannot be transferred outside the European Union,** unless the country has similar protection rights for its data subjects.

Test yourself

1 List five of the principles that data users must obey.

2 Which of these data items would not be relevant for processing a mail-order purchase:

(a) name   **(b)** address   **(c)** credit rating   **(d)** number in family?

Legal aspects

BBC GCSE Check and Test: ICT

Legal aspects

Check the facts

There are **seven data subject rights provided by the Data Protection Act.**

1 The subject can **ask for a copy of all the data** held about him or her. If this request is made, the data user must explain what the data is being used for and how it was obtained.

2 The subject can **prevent any processing of data** that might cause undeserved distress.

3 The subject can **stop data being used for direct marketing.** The request has to be made in writing to the data controller.

4 The subject **can insist that automated decision-making by a computer is not the only method used** to make important decisions about him or her.

5 The subject has the **right to compensation** if he or she is damaged by any breach of the Data Protection Act.

6 The data subject **can have any inaccurate data corrected or erased**.

7 If a data subject thinks personal data is being processed illegally, he or she **can ask the Data Protection Commissioner to check.**

Test yourself

1 Describe five rights given to the data subject by the Data Protection Act.

2 George is tired of people phoning him to try to get him to buy books. What should he do to stop this happening?

Check the facts

Some personal data is exempt from all or part of the Data Protection Act. This means that all or part of the act does not apply.

Full exemption

Full exemption means that **none of the act applies** and **notification that data is being held is not required**. Data used for domestic purposes is always fully exempt.

Partial exemption

Partial exemption means that **at least some of the principles or subject rights do not apply**. Notification that the data is held is still required. Partial exemptions are available for various reasons. Some examples are given in the table below.

Reason	Parts of the act that don't apply
National security	Any of notification, principles and subject rights
Preventing crime and catching criminals	Subject access rights, some of the principles
Data that has to be made public (e.g. electoral register)	Principles concerning passing on data
Research and statistics	Some principles, subject access rights if the subject can't be indented from the results of processing
Confidential references	Subject access rights
Collection and calculation of taxes	Subject access rights, some of the principles

Test yourself

1 What does complete exemption from the Data Protection Act mean?

2 Give three examples of reasons for partial exemption, stating the parts of the act that do not apply.

Legal aspects

BBC GCSE Check and Test: ICT

Legal aspects

Check the facts

Working with computer systems can cause health problems, if care is not taken to ensure the working environment is relatively safe.

Possible problems and methods of prevention are shown in the table below.

Problem	Cause	Prevention
Repetitive strain injury (RSI) to wrists	Repetition of the same movement when typing or using mouse	Provide wrist support, vary work done, take regular breaks, position computer correctly, sit correctly
Headache and eye strain	Glare on screen from lighting, screen flicker; long periods of looking at the screen	Provide anti-glare filter and appropriate lighting; replace defective monitors
Painful neck	Screen at wrong height	Adjust screen height so that the top of the monitor is level with or just below forehead
Backache	Wrong type of chair and lack of foot support	Chair should be adjustable with full back support, provide foot support

It is important for people working with computer systems to take **regular breaks**. It also helps to **vary the work that people do**.

All users should have **regular eye tests**.

Stress can be a problem. **Software should be easy to use** and proper training should be given. **Noise levels** should be kept to a minimum.

Test yourself

1 Why might a person using a computer system all day suffer from eye strain and backache? What can be done to prevent this?

2 What is repetitive strain injury? How can it be prevented?

Check the facts

The **Health and Safety (Display Screen Equipment) Regulations apply to the use of computer equipment at work. Employers, employees and equipment manufacturers all have responsibilities under these regulations.**

Employers have to:

- **Assess each workstation** to make such that there are **no health and safety problems**. If any problems are found, they must be corrected **straight away**.

- **Provide training** for employees, so they know how **to use the equipment properly**.

- Make sure employees **take regular breaks** or **have changes in activity**. A break of ten minutes after two hours should be the minimum.

- Make sure employees have **regular eye tests** and **pay for the tests and glasses** if they are needed.

Employees have to:

- Use the equipment in **the way they have been shown**.

- **Tell employers** if there are problems and **cooperate in solving the problems**. Employees may sometimes move desks and ignore equipment such as footrests and wrist-rests.

Manufacturers have to **produce equipment that meets the requirements**. Screens **must tilt** and **swivel**, and keyboards **must be moveable**.

Test yourself

1 Give three responsibilities employers have to employees who work with computer systems.

2 Why must employees have responsibilities, as well as employers?

Legal aspects

BBC GCSE Check and Test: ICT

Answers

01 Structure of ICT systems

1 Saving a spreadsheet (storage); entering a customer's details (input); working out the average mark (processing); producing a list of pupils on paper (output).

02 System flow charts

1 Movement of data through a system.
2 Data can move both ways, as records can be read and written during the process.

03 Data and information

1 Six, carrots, 30p.
2 Data is raw facts with no meaning; information has meaning because it has a context.

04 Input devices: keyboards

1 d (software running on computer).
2 (any 3): no need to remember prices; easy to change the items sold; faster than typing prices; easy to keep clean.

05 Input devices: pointing devices

1 The software uses the data coming from the mouse in different ways.
2 There is not usually space to use a mouse.

06 Input devices: touch screens, light pens and digitisers

1 **(a)** Digitiser; **(b)** Touch screen.

07 Input devices: image input

1 Scanner.
2 Advantages (any 2): can see picture straight away; only need to keep required pictures; easy to transfer to computer.
Disadvantages: image quality not as good; limited capacity and may not hold all the pictures needed.

08 Input and output of sound

1 Music keyboard, microphone.
2 Microphone.
3 Speech recognition, commentary for presentations.

09 Output devices: screens

1 (a) 9" CRT display for a shop till;
  (b) 14" LCD for a notebook computer;
  (c) 19" CRT display for desktop computer.
2 Viewable size is smaller because the whole of the screen can't be seen. The measurement on the box is the actual size.

10 Output devices: printers

1 (a) Mono laser: black and white, but quality must be good and printer must be fast to produce lots of copies;
(b) Dot matrix: prints multi-part documents;
(c) Colour ink jet: quality not important, as this is an internal notice that won't be displayed for long. Speed not important, as only five copies needed.

11 Storage capacity and memory

1 ROM is non-volatile, RAM is volatile. ROM can't be changed by the user, RAM can be.
2 To hold the start-up instructions.
3 To hold user applications/programs; to hold user data.

12 Storage: magnetic disks

1 On circular tracks divided into sectors.
2 Differences (any 3): hard disk is metal, floppy disk is plastic; hard disk is fixed in drive, floppy is exchangeable; hard disk has a higher capacity than floppy; reading and writing is faster with hard disk than floppy.

13 Storage: magnetic tape

1 High capacity; exchangeable; fast to read and write.
2 Data has to be read in the order in which it was written.

14 Storage: optical media

1 DVD. **2** Distribution of software. **3** CD-R can be written once; data can't be changed; CD-RW can be changed and overwritten.

15 Operating systems

1 Hardware and application software.
2 (any 4): allocate disk space; allocate memory; transfer data; manage security; allocate processor time.
3 User interacts with application software.

16 Multi-tasking systems

1 Appears to run more than one program at same time.
2 Partition memory; keep data for different tasks separate; handle priorities.

17 Multi-user systems

1 A system that lets many users run their programs, apparently at the same time.
2 Keep track of which programs and data belong to which user. Switch programs and data in and out of memory quickly.

18 Data transfer and standard file formats

1 Standard formats: .bmp, .tif, .gif, .jpg, .ico.

2 As a .csv file.

3 .wav indicates to the system that the file contains sound data.

19 User interface: command driven

1 There is a command prompt. The interface is fast. There is little demand on disk space and memory.

2 Advantages: low demand on memory; low demand on storage. **Disadvantage:** user must know commands.

20 User interface: menu driven

1 Menu gives user choices. Little demand on system resources. Uses keyboard input.

2 Cash machine.

21 User interface: graphical

1 Windows, icons, pull-down menus, pointers.

2 User can see everything available. Navigation is by pointing and clicking.

3 Needs a lot of disk space/memory. Slow.

22 Designing a user interface

1 (a) Use restful colours if the interface is to be used for long periods; **(b)** Language must be suitable for level of skill; complex technical language is not appropriate for inexperienced users.

2 Centre of screen, so can easily be seen.

3 Epilepsy, colour-blindness.

23 The system life cycle

1 Analysis, design, implementation, testing, evaluation and maintenance (in this order).

2 Because fixing problems is no longer practical and a new system is needed.

24 Systems analysis

1 Methods are: **(a)** Interview (**advantage:** explore areas of the problem in detail; **disadvantage:** takes a long time); **(b)** Questionnaire (**advantage:** fast, many responses can be collected; **disadvantage:** not all forms are returned); **(c)** Observation (**advantage:** can see what really happens; **disadvantage:** takes a long time).

2 A list of requirements for the new system.

25 System design

1 b (working out record structure), e (planning the layout of a poster).

2 So testing checks the whole system works.

26 Implementation

1 Process of producing the required system.

2 (any 4): setting up input forms for video details; setting up input forms for member details; setting up input forms for loan details; setting up database files for any of videos, members and loans; creating reports for video lists; creating overdue letters; creating mail-merge letters to members.

27 Testing

1 Typical, extreme, erroneous.

2 A letter between B and D (typical); A or E (extreme); a letter between F and Z or a lower-case letter or digit (erroneous).

28 Evaluation

1 Examining how well a system meets the requirements of the user.

2 To find out how successful the system is and if it still meets user requirements.

3 Users have to work with the system.

29 Software maintenance

1 To make the software meet user requirements.

2 Corrective, perfective, adaptive.

3 Corrective. **4** Adaptive.

30 System documentation

1 To explain how the system works for people who will maintain the system. It should include (any 3): details of the structure of every file used; details of all the processing that can be done. Database query designs and spreadsheet formulae must be included here; samples of outputs that can be produced; the testing plan, test data and expected results so tests can be repeated if changes are made; installation instructions, so the software can be installed correctly on the computers.

2 Start-up instructions; instructions for normal use of the system; backup and recovery instructions.

31 Data capture: forms

1 Form must have: suitable prompts for each field; enough boxes for all letters and spaces to be entered (not lines); date format for date of birth; statement of how the data will be used (to meet requirements of Data Protection Act).

2 Limits what can be written.

32 Data capture: OMR

1 Optical Mark Recognition. Machine detects dark marks, transmits data to the computer.
2 Data entry is faster and more accurate than manual methods. The computer adds up the marks.

33 Data capture: OCR

1 Optical Character Recognition. Patterns detected by the reader are matched against stored character patterns. Character codes are built into text in memory.
2 Avoids transposition errors. Faster than typing.
3 Handwriting varies too much.

34 Data capture: MICR

1 Magnetic Ink Character Recognition.
2 More secure, characters can't be changed.

35 Data capture: bar codes

1 (a) Item number; **(b)** Number is used to find the item record in the file, description and price are sent to the till and printed on the receipt; **(c)** Manual input of the bar code number.

36 Magnetic strip and smart cards

1 As a magnetic code/pattern.
2 A smart card can hold more data and can have new data written.
3 Exposure to a magnetic field, heat, bending the card.

37 Data validation: validation tests

1 Making sure data is sensible and reasonable.
2 Validation just makes sure the data can be used by the system.
3 A range check compares the value with maximum allowed and minimum allowed and rejects values outside this range.

38 Data validation: check digits

1 A number worked out from the other digits and added to the end of the data. It is recalculated when the number is input and the digits are compared. If they are the same, the input value is accepted.
2 It will alter the answer, because the digits will be multipled by different amounts

39 Verification checks

1 To make sure data has not been changed when moved from one medium to another.

2 Batch totals: find if records have been missed or repeated. **Entering data twice**: finds mistakes in copying from the source document.

40 Parity checking

1 When data is transmitted along communication links. On transfer from disk to memory.
2 Corruption of data/changes to bit patterns.

41 Data logging: sensors

1 Heat, pressure, light.
2 The computer can't use analogue data.
3 Matching readings to a known scale.
4 So the output makes sense.
5 Read the sensor value at 0 °C, read the value at 100 °C. The computer calculates the temperature for all other sensor readings.

42 Data logging: collecting the data

1 (a) The time between readings;
(b) Total time over which readings are collected.
2 Data is read from sensors; the logging equipment collects this data and then transmits it, using communication links to the computer.

43 Application software

1 Application software is designed to carry out user-related tasks.
2 (a) Spreadsheet; **(b)** Desktop publishing;
(c) Word processing.

44 Application software: development and customisation

1 Configuration changes settings; customisation adds or changes program code.
2 When available packages are unsuitable.

45 Features of a word-processing package

1 Features (any 4): centre the heading, enlarge the font for 'Lost', add a border, add a picture of the dog.

46 Features of a desktop publishing package

1 (any 4): use a decorative heading for title; import photos of the events into picture frames; use subheading styles for different sections; import text files into text frames; flow text between frames.
2 Easier to control the page layout.

47 Features of a drawing package

1 Features (any 5): use shapes to decorate page; use text tools to add text; use decorative line styles and borders to make poster attractive; add clip-art pictures of athletes; change background colour; change the fill style for the background.

2 Easy to move or delete parts of drawing.

48 Features of web-page design software

1 Features (any 4): insert hyperlinks; insert hot spots; change the background; add video clips; animate; preview in web browser; publish to web.

2 Hypertext Markup language (HTML).

49 Spreadsheets

1 D4.

2 = B5*C5.

3 (a) Add a heading for selling price, put in £5.25 next to heading; add a heading for profit, put the formula to calculate profit next to the heading;

(b) Assuming cell D9 is the location of the selling price, formula will be = D9–D8; alternative formula = 5.25–D8.

50 Advantages of using spreadsheets

1 (a) Can try different ideas and spreadsheet will work out new answers. Can have text headings, so he knows what the numbers mean. Can save spreadsheet to work on later. Can print spreadsheet to show everyone how the money is being spent;

(b) May not have a computer available. May not bc familiar with the spreadsheet package.

51 Modelling with a computer

1 Selling price, cost of any item.

2 (a) Put 'Kennel' in cell A7 and 0.25 in B7;

(b) D8.

3 If the rules are wrong, the answer will be wrong.

52 Graphing and charting software

1 (a) Pie chart OR bar chart; **(b)** Label axes, add title, use different colours for fills, add legend.

53 Simulation

1 Cheaper than using a real plane; safer because the simulator can't really crash; repetition is easy.

2 Model may not be correct; the human response may be different in a simulator to the real situation.

54 Files, records and fields

1 A **file** contains data about one topic. A **record** contains all the data about one person or thing. A **field** contains one item of information.

2 A field that uniquely identifies a record. **3** Form, gender.

55 Database field types/record design

1 Text: anything that can be typed in (e.g. cat); **Yes/no**: two possible values, yes/no or true/false (e.g. YES); **Number**: any kind of number (e.g. 125.56); **Date/time**: a date or time (e.g. 13/02/02).

2 People often leave spaces in phone numbers and a text field can hold these. \
3 Surname: text (15 or more); **Forename**: text (15 or more); **School year**: number (automatic); **Form**: text (between 3 and 5); **Gender**: text (1).

56 Fixed- and variable-length records

1 (a) 50; **(b)** 39.

57 Linked files (tables) in databases

1 Avoids data duplication and having to enter same member data each time a book is borrowed.

2 None of the data will be duplicated.

58 Database queries: comparisons

1 Greater than. **2** Like.

59 Simple database queries

1 <field name><comparison><search value>

2 Town equal to 'Bealdrey'/Town like 'Bealdrey'.

60 Complex database queries

1<field name><comparison><search value><OPERATOR><field name><comparison><search value>

2 AND, OR.

3 Town equal to 'Craydon' OR Town equal to 'Bealdrey'.

61 Database queries (linked tables)

1 (a) Supplier code equal to 17;

(b) Supplier code equal to 17 and number in stock less than 100.

Answers

62 Relational database management systems

1 Tasks (any 3): design/set up files/tables; build/use queries; produce/use forms; create/print reports.

63 Mail-merging

1 Using fields from a database to insert data into a word-processed document.
2 Producing personalised advertising material/sending personalised standard letters.

64 Types of processing: batch processing

1 When all data is available, it is processed together, with no further human input.
2 Input data, validate and store in a transaction file. Sort the transaction file. Process the sorted transaction file and the master file to produce the outputs and an updated version of the master file.

65 Real-time and transaction processing

1 Real-time is when outputs are produced fast enough to influence further inputs; **transaction** is when each change is processed as it occurs. Timing not critical.
2 So books that have been returned can be borrowed by other members straight away.

66 Sorting files

1 Moving records to get them into the required order.
2 To organise records in a transaction file into the same order as the master file, ready for batch processing.

67 Merging files

1 When data is input to separate files and a single ordered file is needed.
2 Records are read from each sorted file and are compared and written to the new file in the correct order.

68 File compression

1 Reducing the size of a file by changing the way in which the data is stored.
2 By removing repeating values.

69 File size

1 Because storage costs have fallen.
2 If files have to be put onto a floppy disk. If graphics files are used on web pages. If unwanted database records are not physically deleted by packing the database.

70 Control systems

1 Sensors; the devices that are turned on and off; computer or microprocessor; control program.
2 The system responds quickly enough for outputs to affect further inputs.

71 Physical threats and precautions

1 (a) Physical threats (any 3): water can damage storage media and whole computer systems; heat can damage all storage media; magnetic fields can corrupt data on magnetic media; dirt can damage disks and drives; **(b)** Fire precautions; keep computers away from water; keep media away from magnetic fields; keep media clean.
2 Disks can be scratched or broken.

72 Accidental and deliberate damage

1 Lack of user training; software difficult to use.
2 Users have passwords. Logging off if terminals are left unattended. System locks access after a few wrong attempts to log on.

73 Security of data: viruses

1 A computer program that replicates itself and may damage data. It spreads: through open network connections; attached to e-mail; on infected floppy disks.
2 Use virus-checking software.

74 Transaction-processed applications

1 Copy the main file at the start of the day. Write all transactions to the transaction log file, as each change is made to the main file. Keep the copy with the transaction file.
2 In case the computer system is destroyed.

75 Batch-processed applications

1 In case the Father and Son files are damaged during processing.
2 They are needed to replace a damaged master file.

76 Files on a network file server

1 Daily. **2** Users sometimes take time to discover they have lost data.

77 User ID, levels of access, passwords

1 They control what users can do on the system.
2 They choose words that are easy to guess.

78 Data encryption

1 Changing the data so it can't be understood if it is stolen.
2 Because data can be intercepted during transmission.

79 Local Area Networks (LANs)

1 (any 3): applications and user files can be used on any terminal; central backup; security can be controlled centrally; printers can be shared.
2 Ring, star, bus.

80 Wide Area Networks (WANs)

1 To convert digital computer data to analogue data for transmission on a phone line and to convert it back again at the other end. **2** ISDN, broadband, phone line.

81 E-mail

1 E-mail stays on the receiving mail server until it is retrieved by the recipient.
2 Files (any 3): pictures; documents; databases; programs.

82 E-mail/other methods

1 It is almost instant; it is cheaper than post; it gets to whom it is intended.
2 Sending a parcel containing an object.
3 Multiple copies can all be sent at once; costs less than sending large packages of paper; gets to everyone instantly.

83 The Internet

1 A collection of websites.
2 By an address called a Uniform Resource Locator (URL).

84 The Internet: web browsers

1 Software used to find and display web pages.
2 Refresh to reload pages; history of sites visited recently can be displayed; favourites section stores frequently used URLs

85 The Internet: search engines

1 You may not know the URL of the website, but you know the name of the organisation. You need to find information, but you don't know where to look.
2 When a simple search finds too many pages.
3 If you want to buy something or find a place to visit, you may want somewhere in the UK.

86 The Internet: e-commerce

1 Selling goods and services on the Internet/on-line trading.
2 Banking; booking travel; buying goods.
3 Advantages (any 2): don't have to leave home; can check prices to find the cheapest; goods are delivered. **Disadvantages:** can't see exactly what you're getting; what you want may not be available, and you can't choose something else very easily.

87 The Internet: on-line booking services

1 (a) Cheaper fares; can check availability;
(b) Fewer staff; lower costs; can raise prices, as more seats are booked.

88 Integration of communication devices

1 One device can do several tasks (e.g. phone, camera, Internet access and e-mail).

89 Effects of ICT on society: jobs

1 Increased working from home; new jobs in ICT skills areas; less filing of paper records; check-out staff don't have to add up prices.
2 Work can be sent by e-mail or there can be remote access to company systems.

90 Effects of ICT on society: education

1 Internet is used for research; more ICT presentations produced; e-mail to communicate with other pupils.
2 Recent information available; pictures and text can be copied and pasted into a document or presentation; a great range of information is available.

91 Effects of ICT on society: leisure

1 Internet transmission of sporting events; live transmission of concerts; theme parks use computer simulation for rides.
2 Piracy of music CDs.
3 Hours playing games reduces social contact.

92 Effects of inaccurate data

1 (any 3): data never collected; people give wrong information; mistakes in data entry; accidental deletion. **2** Junk mail delivered for previous occupants; bad credit rating based on postcode, if previous occupier was a bad payer; getting wrong bills, because of data entry errors.

Answers

93 Copyright law and licensing
1 Making extra copies of software for purposes other than backup or installing software on extra computers.
2 He has to buy an extra licence. His single copy is for one computer only.

94 The Computer Misuse Act
1 Making unauthorised access to a computer system.
2 Making unauthorised access to computer programs or data. Making unauthorised access with the intention to commit a further crime. Making unauthorised modifications to programs or data.

95 The Data Protection Act: introduction
1 What data they hold. What they use the data for. Where they get the data. Who the data may be passed on to.
2 (any 3): racial or ethnic origin; religious beliefs; political views; health; criminal record; sexual preferences; trade union membership.
3 To control the way in which personal data about living people can be collected and used.

96 The data protection principles
1 **Principles** (any 5): Personal data: must be collected and processed fairly and lawfully. It can only be processed if certain conditions are met; must be obtained for specific purposes and can't be used for other purposes; must be adequate, relevant and not excessive for the purpose for which it is obtained; must be accurate and must be kept up to date; must not be kept for longer than necessary. It must be deleted or destroyed when it is no longer needed; must be processed with regard to the rights of the data subject; must be kept secure and safe from accidental or deliberate damage; cannot be transferred outside the EU, unless the country has similar protection of the rights of data subjects. **2** d (number in family).

97 Data subject rights
1 **Rights** (any 5): The subject can: ask for a copy of all the data held about him or her. If this request is made ,the data user must explain what the data is being used for and how it was obtained; prevent any processing of data that might cause undeserved distress; stop data being used for direct marketing. The request has to be made in writing to the data controller; insist that automated decision-making by a computer is not the only method used to make important decisions about him or her; get compensation if he or she is damaged by any breach of the Data Protection Act; The data subject can: have any inaccurate data corrected or erased; ask the Data Protection Commissioner to check, if he or she thinks personal data is being processed illegally.
2 Request the data controller of the company involved to stop using personal data in this way.

98 The Data Protection Act: exemptions
1 The Act does not apply and there is no need to notify.
2 **Reasons for partial exemption** (any 3): National security (any of notification, principles and subject rights); preventing crime and catching criminals (subject access rights, some of the principles); data that has to be made public, e.g. electoral register, (principles concerning passing on data); research and statistics (some principles, subject access rights, if the subject can't be identified from the results of processing); confidential references (subject access rights); collection and calculation of taxes (subject access rights, some of the principles).

99 Health and safety issues
1 Eye strain caused by glare on screen, screen flicker, long periods looking at the screen. Prevented by using anti-glare screen, better monitor, taking breaks. Backache caused by wrong type of chair, no foot support. Prevented by providing adjustable chair and foot support.
2 Damage caused by constant repetition of the same movement. Prevented by use of wrist support.

100 Health and Safety Regulations
1 **Employer responsibilities** (any 3): assess work stations and fix problems; provide training; make sure breaks are taken; pay for eye tests and glasses.
2 If they ignore what they are told to do, health problems aren't the employer's fault.